Let Them Shine

D1565449

LET THEM SHINE

Inspiring Stories of Empowering Young Children

Michael Alan Haggood, EdD

Redleaf Press®
www.redleafpress.org
800-423-8309

Published by Redleaf Press
10 Yorkton Court
St. Paul, MN 55117
www.redleafpress.org

First edition 2020
Cover design: Erin Kirk New
Cover photograph: iStock.com/SDI Productions
Interior design: Douglas Schmitz
Typeset in Janson Text
Printed in the United States of America
27 26 25 24 23 22 21 20   1 2 3 4 5 6 7 8

Library of Congress Cataloging-in-Publication Data
Names: Haggood, Michael Alan, author.
Title: Let them shine : inspiring stories of empowering young children /
    Michael Alan Haggood, EdD.
Description: First edition. | St. Paul, MN : Redleaf Press, 2020. |
    Includes bibliographical references. | Summary: "Michael wrote this book
    to help educators nurture the spark or light in each child, no matter
    their circumstances. After all, "No child can learn from you if they
    feel you are not interested in them." He highlights the crucial and
    pivotal role educators play in children's lives and how their actions
    often have lifelong effects on the children in their care. "— Provided by publisher.
Identifiers: LCCN 2019030538 (print) | LCCN 2019030539 (ebook) | ISBN
    9781605547213 (paperback) | ISBN 9781605547220 (ebook)
Subjects: LCSH: Motivation in education.
Classification: LCC LB1065 .H25 2020 (print) | LCC LB1065 (ebook) | DDC
    370.154—dc23
LC record available at https://lccn.loc.gov/2019030538
LC ebook record available at https://lccn.loc.gov/2019030539

Printed on acid-free paper

When I was young, I thought electricity—and all other light—came from a lighthouse. I don't know how I first learned about lighthouses, but I firmly believed that, no matter the distance, all light could be made bright from this one place. My mother is my lighthouse. Everything good in my life is because of her unconditional love, unwavering teachings, and aligned guidance. Yes, I am responsible for my actions, but my dutiful motivation and inspiring kindness is fueled by her.

People were mean to her in this world, and she continued to be courageous enough to love. Roberta Ann Webb Haggood Rinehart, I salute you and pay homage to your light. The light you have given me is the best gift ever. Your effect on my life has always been light. Yes, we are separated by distance, but I feel you constantly maneuvering my life in dramatic ways.

Contents

Acknowledgments

To Redleaf Press staff, for recognizing my experiential stories as learning for others.

To my chosen children (Ebonie, Taurean, Dontavious, Emmanuel, and Fateemah), for your love and trust.

To Scott, Phil, and Patrice, for their unwavering support of their crazy little brother.

To Britney and Braxton, who remind me of my mother's smile when I see them.

To Bishop Carl Bean, for affecting millions through your teachings of freedom, self-love, and peace.

To Holly Elissa Bruno, for being an angel.

To Abraham Hicks, for teaching "allowing."

To Vivica A. Fox, for challenging me to be great past others' expectations.

To Carol Fujita, for having the courage to appreciate life.

To Dr. Ayanna Davis, for daily and weekly insights of inspiration.

To Reverend Freda Lenoix, for always guiding others to light.

To Xavier Boykin, for allowing me to love.

To Tristen Day, Yvette Anderson, Donna Washington, and Candie Childress, for your sisterly love.

To my aunts, cousins, nieces, and nephews, for loving me unconditionally.

To my godchildren, Bobby, Ray, Chris, Sammy, Abby, and Tierra, for letting your light shine.

To Justin Childress, for your amazing photographic skill.

To Yetive Lowery, for my best example of educational empowerment.

To Anthony Ball, for your dutiful example of glass half full.

To Tracy Kennedy, for showing me freedom.

To the Los Angeles Unified School District, California Director Mentor Program, CSUDH, and National University for allowing me to facilitate the growth of thousands of early education teachers, protégés, mentees, and students.

To my fellow professional educators, who persist in the face of nonrecognition from society that early education is a key to lifelong success.

To the countless angels (and in particular Dad and Babe) who guide my path.

And lastly to Manny, for filling my heart!

Introduction

"This little light of mine, I'm gonna let it shine." Many are familiar with this tune and its powerful message. This song reminds us that every child is shining a light. Every child wants to share their light.

How does one preserve that spark, that light in children? Adults must be purposeful when they interact with children. It is true that a child can change their life trajectory through education, and it's also true that one person's actions can have a lasting, positive effect on a child. The best strategy to empower children to learn from you is to build a strong relationship with them. The relationship between teacher and child or parent and child must be one in which the child truly believes you care about their well-being. Nothing fosters this development faster than when you support the social-emotional development of the children you teach and care for.

Helping teachers nurture the light in their students was not my only reason for writing this book. I also wrote it for the educator who needs a boost, a recharge of some kind to get them going again. Do you ever wonder what happened to that "called" notion you felt when you got your initial teaching assignment? Or perhaps you're an administrator who has lost your inspiration and just wants to make it to retirement. Reclaim your passion! My wish for you is to rekindle your heartfelt desire to affect children's lives for the better. These stories may remind you of your own special memories, like the gift of seeing a child read for the first time or the gratification you felt when you helped a shy student overcome their fear. Teachers, caregivers, social workers, coaches, mentors, and others who work with young children have all experienced special moments when their guidance and support has affected a child so positively that it made their heart smile.

I also hope this book appeals to parents, because you play a crucial role in helping your child's light shine. My greatest joy in life is being the father of five wonderful children, each adopted in love and parented differently based on their individual needs. There is more than one way to parent your child. I believe that choice is great. However, I don't allow my child to put her hand on the stove to test its hotness after I warn against it. I firmly state the reason why the stove is hot and how touching it will hurt. Old-school parenting is great, but I do not expect children to simply obey and not touch the stove "because I said so." This will create a decision-deficit adult. Instead, I explain my reasoning, which encourages internal discipline and does not deter the child's power of choice in future decision-making or their free will. As you can see, I choose to use a combination of parenting styles, for neither will work in isolation of the other.

How do we develop our individual parenting styles? Remembering how we were parented, coupled with observing other parents, typically shapes our basic notions of parenting. Old-school parenting gets its name and definition from this very basis. We have all heard the claim "I'm old school." This phrase runs rampant in many schools and homes where teachers and parents wear the three words as a badge of honor. Then there are the progressives: choice is everything. They believe that giving a child a choice is the best way to parent.

I grew up in one household with two different parenting styles. My dad was certainly old school, and my mom leaned on the side of choice. I hesitate to say that age and race (my mom, Scottish American, and my dad, African American) had an important part to play in this difference. However, I do know my upbringing contributed culturally to who I am today, and it definitely affected my parenting style and how I communicate with children. I am a balance of each of my parents and their parenting styles. Overall I believe that we each develop our parenting style as a result of witnessing others and, more often than not, trial-and-error experiences.

I can still recall the day my son threw a major fit in a Blockbuster video store. I couldn't believe it. There he was, sprawled out on the floor kicking and screaming because I told him that a movie he wanted to watch was for adults and not children. I was embarrassed because other parents in the store were witnessing his tantrum. I realized that if handled well, this unfortunate incident did not have to happen again. As a matter of fact, I remember thinking this would be the last time this would occur if I handled this situation correctly.

I kneeled down and got directly in my son's face. With a serious look and the firmest whisper I could muster, I said, "You've got three seconds to get up off that floor." Now imagine there is a pause between each word to add significance to the moment: "You've . . . got . . . three . . . seconds . . . to . . . get . . . up . . . off . . . that . . . floor."

Once my son got off the floor, I gave him a choice. "Our day at the store is over. Maybe we can come again tomorrow because we are not having fun anymore, and that is what this was all about. You need to apologize to the manager of this store. We will not be coming back unless you apologize. You have a choice."

Looking back I realize this was a moment where I definitely had to use both parenting styles to resolve the situation. This balance between progressive and old-school parenting has worked well for me over the years, both as a parent and as a professional. I found it extremely effective when I was a teacher and even more so now that I am a principal.

This is just one story I want to share with you. The other stories in this book are about empowering children, celebrating our differences, strengthening relationships, developing empathy, and more. I hope these stories will make your heart dance, smile, and perhaps even cry!

When you explore the moments when children have baffled, surprised, and even shocked me, you may be reminded of your own experiences and how a child's behavior triggered a memorable reaction from you. Every story in this book is true. I lived them. The amazing and sometimes terrifying experiences I have faced have shaped my passion and allowed me to serve on behalf of countless children and their families.

Many chapters will challenge you to think about how you would react if placed in a similar situation. At the end of each chapter, you will find reflection questions and activities. The reflection questions will ask you to call upon your own experiences with the children in your life. You will also find learning objectives and activities, which can be adapted to the needs and circumstances of those in your care. It is my hope that you will add these activities to your educational tool kit.

As a black gay man, proud father of five, and fearless educator who has been serving the needs of children, families, and teachers in the Los Angeles area for thirty-four years, I felt compelled to share my educational journey with you. I have served as an aide, teacher, assistant principal, parent, special needs coordinator, human relations director, professor, principal, and president of countless educational organizations. In each of these positions, I was reminded that educators are beacons of light. Ultimately it is our responsibility to nurture the light in every child placed in our care and to appreciate being part of their journey. This book is for you. We are leaving the light on for you so that you empower children to shine!

1 Empowering Students: Teacher's Pet

HAVE YOU EVER FELT so special that your heart lit up? A moment when you felt like your heart tank was full? It's like that warm feeling you get in your stomach when you undergo a medical procedure and drink that pink milk to see your insides. That's the feeling I get whenever I think of my third-grade teacher, Ms. Bream. She made me feel so special, and she made me realize that the best gift any parent or teacher can give a child is the gift of empowerment.

Before the third grade, I hated school. There were no mixed emotions—I *hated* school. As I walked to school each day in the same worn-out jeans and Converse tennis shoes, I would conjure up visions of being sent to the principal's office. Unfortunately a trip to his office was not an unusual occurrence for me. I had a habit of speaking my mind, and it was my mouth that would get me into the most trouble.

My first- and second-grade teachers just didn't like me; at least that's what I believed at the time. I sort of understood why they felt this way. Even I began to wonder why I could not keep my mouth shut. "Be quiet, Michael," was said to me so often that I would even hear those words being spoken to me in my dreams. Yes, I was mouthy, talkative, and possibly even brash, but I was never disrespectful or uncontrollable. I wasn't aggressive in a bad way, which meant that there was hope for me.

These were the days when collaborative grouping, conversational talk, and peer sharing were nonexistent. Classrooms were regimented, and sitting at our desks in nice, neat rows waiting for either a lecture or a test was commonplace. Before third grade, I would count the minutes until recess or PE, any moment that allowed me to get out of that chair. I knew I was smart. I would score toward the head of the class without even really listening. School to me was a real punishment, and I believed that I would just have to endure the painful torture until I was eighteen.

The only bright spot during that time in my life was my mom. She believed that this mouth of mine would eventually take me places. If it hadn't been for her love, wisdom, and guidance during this difficult period, my light may have eventually dwindled away to nothing. Fortunately she realized my greatest weakness had the potential to be my greatest strength. My mom was my greatest supporter, and there was no way she was going to let someone break my spirit. She would say things like "Don't worry, Michael. The world is not ready for you yet" and "You will make money with that mouth of yours; they will see."

Then God sent Ms. Bream to the rescue. OMG! She was unlike any teacher I had ever met. As she approached our class at the beginning of my third-grade year, I was in awe. Not only was she physically beautiful (tall, pretty, and Raquel Welch–like), she had a pleasant, cheerful manner. After all these were the days of old-school behavior modification. Many teachers went around quoting their badge of honor: "Those kids better not mess with me. I'm old school." What they really meant, in my opinion, was, "I need an excuse for being mean." Ms. Bream wasn't that kind of teacher.

It wasn't just her beauty or her pleasant disposition that inspired me. Ms. Bream was the first person on the planet, other than my mom, who made me feel special. So special that I began to believe that I would be someone important in this world. She would say wonderful things about me to me and the other children. She called me a kickball champion and the best speller in class, and she talked about how wonderful it was that I had strong opinions. She made my aggressive traits seem refreshing when they had only been seen as problematic for my first- and second-grade teachers. Often she would find some random reason to compliment me. Or at least it felt random. Later I would find out that it wasn't random at all.

Many years later, I had just returned home to Los Angeles from military service at Fort Riley, Kansas, where I had earned an educational college bonus to pay for my teaching degree at the University of California at Dominguez Hills. I didn't know at the time that one day I would be teaching there as a faculty professor, and I also had no idea that I was about to have a chance encounter with Ms. Bream that would forever shape my hopes and dreams for the future. About two weeks after I returned home, my cousin Tracy and I ran into Ms. Bream at Ralph's market near my home. Before this chance meeting, I often thought about Ms. Bream and asked myself, "How could one person have such an effect on another?" I wanted to be Ms. Bream. I wanted to have that same effect on children's lives. How had she done it? She made me feel relevant, visible, and included. My love for learning and school started because of her. And there I was, years later, running into her in Ralph's. She was still beautiful and radiant and smiling ever so brightly at me with pride. My cheeks ached from smiling so widely.

In an attempt to show my cousin Tracy how important this moment was for me, I crowed, "Ms. Bream, tell him, please, how special I was and how I was your favorite student."

The unexpected response just about killed me. Ms. Bream simply said, "You were not my favorite."

Right there in Ralph's market, I could have just laid down and died. Shocked I began to stutter, "Uh-uh-what-wah-wah that does not make sense. All those things you said about me."

"Yes," replied Ms. Bream. "They were true."

"What about when you brought my report card to my home and we had pizza? What about all the times I got chosen to have lunch and be line leader and supply clerk and office monitor? And, oh yeah, my birthday. You made a really big deal out of it that year. I remember, don't you?"

"Yes, Michael, I remember," Ms. Bream said patiently. "Now that you are grown, I'll let you in on a big secret of mine. Remember the Dixie riddle cup that would sit on my desk? It had popsicle sticks in it, and they had numbers on them."

"Yes, I kind of remember that," I said, not sure what the popsicle sticks had to do with anything.

"Kids always wondered what they were for, and I would respond that the district had us keep them there for attendance. Well that is not what they were for. You see, at the end of each stick was a number from one to thirty-two. Each corresponding number represented one of my students. If you remember, I would take two sticks and place them on my desk every other Monday. So simply stated, each student's stick got a turn during the year being picked out of the cup. And here is the secret, Michael. For those two weeks, I would get the opportunity to spoil those two children rotten. Yes, they would be line leader, class reader, ball monitor . . . any responsibility I could think of would be theirs for those two weeks. I would look for their strengths and talents and lavish them with as much verbal praise as their hearts and minds could take. And yes, lunchtime dates with the teacher and even visits to the home were done to show each child that they were important and special. Michael, all my children are my favorite. You remember how you felt that year in my class? All my students feel that way."

Even though it was a shock to hear that I wasn't Ms. Bream's favorite student after all, my best memory of school is and always will be Ms. Bream. Her awe-inspiring treatment of me was a gift to me and to each child in her class. My relationship with Ms. Bream and her ability to make children feel special is the reason I am an educator today! The benefits of her teaching strategy were unknown to me until I became an adult and a teacher myself.

Ms. Bream didn't just make me feel special. She also empowered me. Empowerment is based on the idea that building a child's skills, resources, authority, opportunity, and motivation—as well as holding them accountable for the outcomes of their actions—will contribute to their competence and self-satisfaction. Ms. Bream modeled the ideal of empowerment each day. Through her example, she taught me patience, responsibility, and, because she never bailed me out, resilience. I learned that guessing and taking risks were preferred over giving up. Most of all, I learned that each person has value based on how she valued me and each of my classmates.

Inspiring and motivational people are all around us, and luckily there are many Ms. Breams in this world. Whether a librarian, teacher, bus driver, or pastor, they all have one thing in common: they believe that all children have special talents that should be noticed and nurtured so they will do well in school and in their adult lives.

It's important for educators to remember to celebrate each child's unique gifts. In my professional experience, I have seen an increased focus on standardized test scores in the nation's schools, and in my opinion, it can lead to educators neglecting other types of student intelligence. Art, music, and many other subjects that highlight the various strengths a child may possess are not a consideration under most present-day assessments. Unfortunately a child's interest in art, music, or extracurricular activities does not carry the same weight of importance as a high test score. As I look back at the schools that I have served as a teacher and administrator, I notice the inequity of students of color admitted to advanced-placement classes and gifted-identification processes. Instead of following this trend of statewide testing importance, my hope is that early childhood education continues to respect and value the whole-child approach. This helps children feel special and empowered, regardless of their strengths.

Preschool teachers will tell you that children as early as two and three years old demonstrate difficulty in showing their abilities. A shy child with an array of talents may sit during a directed lesson and not share their skills unless the teacher finds ways to prompt their participation. The best schools use broader methods to identify children in classrooms, theaters, and playgrounds so that "giftedness" is redefined as a specialized ability in a given area. All children possess these abilities to varying degrees.

Families can also play an important part in helping children develop their talents. Promoting and identifying a child's special abilities and sharing them with the school and the teacher can be the best way for a parent to show advocacy. Recognizing and supporting children's individual talents should be done as early as possible so they can reach their full potential. Additionally all parents can help their child learn, which can provide insight into their child's special abilities. Having a parent who has a history of academic success may be beneficial, but it is not a prerequisite for helping a child learn and improve in school.

When assisting my own children with their studies, I always ensured there was a quiet learning space in my home. It links school to home for a child and simultaneously sends them a message that learning takes place everywhere you go. I was also an investigative parent with my own children. When it came to their schoolwork, I wanted to know what they were learning. If they appeared to be unsure or were too vague in their responses, I would make it my business to communicate my concerns to their teachers. Open communication between families and those who care for and teach our children should always be encouraged. This is easier now more than ever considering email is often the preferred method of communication between parent and teacher.

When I must confront a child who has exhibited bad behavior or poor school performance, one strategy I always rely on is telling them how disappointed I am. This phrase seems to tug at their heartstrings. Of course the guilt a child feels for disappointing you will only be evident if you've given them encouragement and consistent positive praise along the way. This practice sets the tone; creating clear expectations for the children in your care will empower them and make them feel valued.

Thankfully I discovered what teaching has always been all about for me: a relationship. There are many educators and educational theorists who coin phrases like "You can't teach a child anything if they think you don't like them or they don't like you." I wholeheartedly agree with the message in this phrase, and it makes me think of my wonderful time as a student in Ms. Bream's classroom. The educational strategy of the Dixie cup and popsicle sticks has stayed with me throughout my teaching and administrative career. Whether I am teaching adult students at the university, administering and assisting teachers in the classroom at my preschools, or mentoring youth and young adults in my professional and personal life, I will always remember Ms. Bream's intention and influence as I pay it forward.

Self-Confidence

When you give children responsibilities in the classroom, you are not only helping them build self-esteem, but you are also helping them build life skills. Everyday tasks like watering the plants, straightening up, and organizing the work or play area are all positive and worthwhile activities.

Children need opportunities to demonstrate their competence and feel that their contribution is valuable. In the home, that means asking them, even when they're toddlers. Helping with meal preparation, setting the table, folding laundry, and making beds are simple activities children can handle.

If you have a young child or even an older child who is having difficulty believing in themselves, this simple yet powerful activity can be very helpful. On a sticky note, write an inspirational note with a positive word or phrase about the child and attach it to a mirror where they will see it. If you are using this activity in the classroom, make sure you are using shatterproof mirrors that are classroom safe. What could be a better way to start the day than getting praise and affirmation from others?

A surefire way to build self-esteem and improve a child's decision-making skills is to ask them what special activity they would like to take part in during free or playtime. You can offer them a list of different activities to choose from, and once they make their decision, you can make them feel even more special by asking them to help you plan the activity they chose.

Expose the children in your care to activities outside the classroom. Take them to places where they can experience different learning environments. Bookstores, neighborhood libraries, and museums offer wonderful opportunities for stories and adventures.

Reflections

☼ How have your past relationships with teachers shaped your current teaching strategies?

☼ How have your teaching strategies evolved over time?

☼ What do you want your students to remember most about you?

☼ How well do you know the children in your care?

☼ What approach do you take when it comes to empowering your students?

☼ How are you helping the children in your care develop a positive identity?

☼ How do you use positive praise as a motivator for students?

☼ How are you embracing diverse teaching strategies for diverse learners?

2 Sharing Experiences: The Giving Tree

WHY DO WE GIVE? My acts of giving and the reasons why I give have not come without some investigative self-reflection. I've thought about this a lot. Years ago I remember my cousin Tracy and I debating the concept of giving and whether the biggest benefit went to the receiver or the giver. Tracy would often tell family members that he would really prefer it if they would just ask him what he wanted for Christmas. He didn't appreciate when someone tried to surprise him with a gift if there was a chance they would get him something he might not want. If I am honest, I enjoy giving because it makes me feel good. Yes, I get great pleasure in seeing the delight on someone's face who has just received a gift from me; it warms my heart.

My enthusiasm for giving affects both my personal and professional lives. You may be familiar with Shel Silverstein's book *The Giving Tree*. To say this book made an impact on my life is an understatement. This children's book not only helped me teach my students important life lessons, but it also inspired me to give. What's more, I believe it led to the adoption of my first son, Emmanuel.

It's amazing to think that one book that promotes the concept of sharing changed the direction of my life. In the spring of 1996, one of the reading options for the literacy portion of the day was *The Giving Tree*. Our school district was linked into "whole language reading" as a strategy for increasing reading literacy. Whole language at the time was a method the district used to teach reading and writing. Rather than utilizing the phonics method, it emphasized learning whole words and phrases and then putting them into meaningful context or themes for the students. I thought the theme of giving would be a good choice. What began with a simple interest in using a book for increasing literacy resulted in much more.

For those unfamiliar with *The Giving Tree*, it is a story about the relationship between a tree and a boy. The tree's unconditional love for the boy is evident throughout the story. She wants to please him whenever she can. When he is little, the tree demonstrates her giving nature by letting the boy climb her trunk, eat her apples, and swing from her boughs. As time goes by and the boy grows, he is no longer satisfied with their relationship. He demands more from the tree. He wants her to give him something tangible, something that has material value. In an effort to satisfy the boy, the tree consents and gives him parts of herself that she can never replace. She is happy to sacrifice herself for the boy because she cares deeply for him and finds joy in giving him what he wants. However, near the end of the story, the tree and the boy realize there are negative consequences for their actions. Over the years, the tree gives the boy everything she possibly can, until all that is left of this majestic tree is her stump. Her happiness wanes. The boy no longer thinks about visiting her because she has nothing left of value for him to take. The curious, playful boy from the past is gone. As a tired, lonely old man, he goes to visit the tree to ask her for one last gift, "a quiet place to sit and rest." Given the opportunity to give once more, "the Tree was happy."

The book was an amazing experience for my class. I say "experience" because that is what it turned into. We were all so inspired by the book that for the month of May, my classroom literally transformed into the Giving Tree. Instructional activities supported the theme as well. A huge visual papier-mâché tree was constructed, and the branches covered our ceiling and fanned out across our classroom.

Each day my students were reminded of the giving theme through our reading or literacy work. The students participated in "giving day Fridays," when children got a turn to sit in the middle of a class circle and receive positive compliments from each of their peers. I can vividly recall a student, Kendra, and her face on one particular Friday. Her smile was so wide she seemed about to explode from the onslaught of kind words said to her by her classmates. There were also "helpful Mondays," when select students were given responsibilities to ensure that the day ran smoothly. I remember another student, Calvin, and the pride in his stance as he stuck his chest out when he was told that he was the computer monitor for each Monday of the month. Parents also contributed to the month's theme by donating items from home. It was a special month.

I believe that nothing happens by accident. This concept of giving began to affect my personal life as well. A friend of mine visited my home during the month of May, and as we engaged in frivolous conversation, she asked me, "Hey, are you still interested in being a dad?" "Of course," I responded. She then told me of a lesbian couple she knew who had just adopted a baby. I was amazed because at the time, gay people becoming parents seemed like a foreign concept. However, I yearned to give of myself as a parent.

My friend then encouraged me to adopt, knowing that my dream was to be a dad and raise a child. After asking thousands of questions, I decided to give it a shot. I went to the Adoptions First in Northridge, California, to complete an application of interest. It reminded me of showing up for a job interview when you already know you won't get an offer but feeling compelled to try anyway.

Everything about the visit told me that my dream was impossible. Pictures of lily-white families with their new infants graced the walls. I didn't see one person of color. In that moment, I realized the lesbian couple that had inspired my friend and me must have been lily white too. Being black and gay, I thought I had no chance.

Why was I here? More embarrassment followed when I glanced over the agency's application. Should I reveal everything? Although I was told this agency was gay friendly, I was skeptical because the church I attended at the time stated they were gay friendly, yet rejection of gay people did occur. It scared me. After completing the application truthfully, not holding back anything, I was sure nothing would come of it. I was afraid this wasn't going to be my path to fatherhood after all. But God had other plans, and boy was I wrong.

The call came in July 1996, only three months after visiting the agency and submitting an application. I was shocked because I had all but forgotten about the agency and the chance to become a father. The agency told me that a mother had selected me out of five potential applicants and wanted to meet me to discuss the possibility of adopting her baby. I could not believe that a parent would choose me to adopt their child; I was bewildered but honored.

I asked my good friend Melissa to go with me to the hospital. We arrived at Long Beach Memorial Hospital with anxious anticipation. My heart felt as if it was about to explode. Waiting in the elevator with Marci, heading to a nursery to meet my potential child, was beyond my wildest dreams. I also could not have imagined the nurses' heartfelt greetings as the elevator doors opened. When I told them why I was there, they looked at me with such love that I began to cry.

Then like Moses parting the sea, the nurses began to separate as the head nurse walked toward me and placed a beautiful baby boy in my arms. As I held him I wondered how one remembers who they once were, as innocent as the baby I was holding. Wrapped in a blanket, he gave off a sweet scent that overpowered me. I felt this calling, not to something tangible but to the next phase of my life. I felt out of step with it, though. This newness, like this baby, was a change that seemed far away, but I knew it was coming and I relaxed in it, bathed in it, and smiled. I knew in this moment that I was feeling the creator of all worlds and what it must have felt when it blew breath and created such magnificence in this world.

This moment of utter acceptance and submission precipitated what can only be explained as God taking every wheel in my life. First I realized that I had not prepared for a baby. I had nothing. No crib, no bottles, no formula (which I didn't even know babies needed at the time), nothing. It was during this moment of quiet panic that I looked out the window and saw a Walmart. Marci told me not to worry as she left to purchase a crib. The nurses informed me that they had packed blankets and enough formula, diapers, and bottles for a month to help me get started. They said it wasn't every day that they got the chance to help a single man adopt a baby. I wondered if they had gotten the chance to meet this beautiful baby boy's mother. I speculated that if they had, they were probably very empathetic to her, as they were sharing so much love and empathy with the baby and me.

As we arrived at my fourplex apartment, I was overwhelmed with gratitude. This was no toy, I realized. This was a human being. I cried uncontrollably, thankful that my new baby was asleep. As my family and close friends began to learn what happened, the phone calls started coming in. After a while, I decided to stop answering so that I could be present in the moment.

As I focused on what seemed like a dream to me, I realized a cycle of giving, which started with a book, had played a significant part in this exact moment. Over the next two weeks, an amazing group of people swarmed my house and bestowed upon me an incredible amount of love and gifts. I wish I could say the next two weeks went off without a hitch. However, with only my mom to model parenthood for me, I was probably not the most qualified applicant to be this baby's parent. First I tightly wrapped my beautiful baby in a blanket (based on directions that the nurses gave me) and almost suffocated him. It was my neighbor, Carol, who exclaimed that wrapping him too tightly could kill him. Then my next mistake in this comedy of errors (although it really wasn't funny at the time) was almost unbearable. I fed my new baby boy formula straight from the can. Yes, no chaser. No milk, no water, just straight from the can. I know! Every mother reading this right now could just kill me. Baby boy pooped for days on days on days.

Although I had always wanted to be a father, I knew it would be a sacrifice. What I did not understand then was the reciprocal process of giving. Experience has always been my best teacher. Giving, and making people you love happy, can be more rewarding than receiving any gift. To make people you love happy, you may need to give something up that is important to you. I have come to learn that the reciprocal act of giving is real. Giving without expecting anything in return has usually had a magical ending for me. Like some whimsical spiritual philosophy that I know nothing about, whenever I have given in life, I have always received much more in return.

Of course the reciprocal giving tree of this beautiful baby boy would have been enough for me, but my receiving was just starting. The same angel friend responsible for my going to the agency in the first place had come over for a visit. Astonished at how I was holding up as a single father but knowing that I was overwhelmed, she suggested that I take a day off and let her watch the baby. She then told me about a game show that was holding auditions nearby. I was a fan of game shows and thrilled at the idea of getting out of the house, so I went. Two weeks later, I was told that I would be a contestant on the show.

I was riding the energy of giving, and it must have resonated through my pores because everything—and I mean everything—was set up for me to win. The show was called *Majority Rules*, and the way to win was to have a strong opinion about something and be able to sway others to agree with you. I have plenty of opinions. Strong opinions? I definitely have those too.

The show is designed so that contestants voted on one another's opinions. This was revealed after a morning breakfast where players were unaware that they were actually meeting the very people who would control their fate. Of course the nicer you were, the better your chances were that these same people would like you and thus like what you had to say.

After the morning continental breakfast, I was seated next to a lady who reminded me so much of my mother that I began to believe there was a reason I had been selected to be on this show. Then, as forty-nine other contestants were seated around me, the first question was offered: "What is your favorite television show and why?" I rang my buzzer and the lights around my chair began to glow. I answered *Melrose Place*. Another contestant rang in and said *Hawaii Five-O*. I was awarded 86 percent of the audience's votes.

For the next two hours, I felt like I was on some sort of train, but I wasn't driving. With each question, I felt the excitement and adrenaline running through my veins; it was overwhelming. Even the questions they asked seemed to imply I was destined to be on the show, as I had strong opinions about all of them. What is your favorite show and why? What do men hate to do the most? What is your dream profession? These conversational questions, coupled with my ability to ad lib, were right up my alley.

I ended up winning the first two shows. I drove home with the most appreciative cry ever, anticipating telling my family what had happened. It was pure luck that my friend encouraged me to try out for that show. Luck soon turned into divinity, because I ended up winning $24,200, which allowed me to pay for my baby boy's entire adoption.

Looking back I never would have imagined that my choosing a book as a project theme for my classroom would be the catalyst for such giving and ultimate receiving in my life. It is the best example that I have of experiencing our Creator in all of its wisdom. I believe that my decision to step up and give an incredible child a home was rewarded, as it was a miracle that I showed up on a game show three weeks later and won enough money to pay for his adoption (especially considering that I knew I would struggle to pay for his adoption).

The Giving Tree is not just a book about a boy learning about giving. It's also a lesson that words in books can be lived. They are expressions and offerings for the reader to choose to follow or deny and reject. I was constantly reminded of a book's potential to significantly affect a person's life as I witnessed my amazing baby boy grow to become a beautiful, kind, considerate, and brilliant twenty-one-year-old young man.

The concept of giving is such an important and assessable factor for social-emotional readiness in the preschool years, and it may even be a subconscious reason why I transferred from elementary to early education. Children struggle with giving in the early years. However, a child can be taught to understand some basic rules, such as sharing their toys, and this early introduction to giving has the potential to positively affect their entire life.

Sharing is a skillset that, if learned early, will benefit every child. During the preschool years, your child is becoming capable of understanding the pleasure of giving. But it is not until they see the benefits of sharing that they will freely choose to do so. One benefit they can experience is the joy of interaction with a playmate or family member. They will find that it is more fun to share a toy with someone than to have it all to themselves. That is because they are developing a sense of self in relation to others. In doing so, they are beginning to understand the importance of giving and community.

Though it can be frustrating and even embarrassing at times, difficulty sharing is a common behavior for toddlers as well as older children. Fortunately you can teach your little one to share using a variety of techniques. I have found the best strategy for empowering young children to give is to lead by example. Children are always watching adults and receive action cues on how to handle situations that they may not be ready for. Let children see you actively sharing, and it will guide their thinking as well.

One of the best times to model giving is during the holidays (although you can certainly do this any time of the year). A tradition in my home is to give to others during this time of year. One of the proudest moments I have had in my life was watching my daughter Ebonie coordinate the giving of holiday items to a homeless shelter in downtown Los Angeles a few years ago. Watching the faces of homeless recipients and their expressions of gratitude was rewarding enough, but to know that my daughter may have been inspired to give because of something she had learned in my home brought me to tears.

Giving is a very personal thing for everyone. Some give out of guilt, some out of obligation, and some just for pure pleasure—there are many different reasons. Here are three fundamental reasons why I believe giving soothes the soul:

1. **You become less self-absorbed.** Being truly aware of someone else's needs not only teaches us about the gift of giving, but it also helps us understand the importance of empathy. During the act of giving, the giver is no longer focused on self. Problems, issues, or situations that would normally be on your mind soon dissipate.

2. **The returns are huge.** I believe that the more you give, the more you will receive. Giving to others is commendable, which is why it's important for educators to see themselves as givers. I want this to be your legacy. Educators have great influence. You have the ability

to change the world. Sometimes it may be in small ways, and sometimes it may be in astronomical ways.

3. **You make a difference.** Even when you intend your giving for
   many but it ends up being for only one, you're still making a difference. Loren Eiseley's *The Star Thrower* illustrates this best in the
   story of an elderly man who sees a young man throwing beached
   starfish back into the ocean. The old man tells the young man he's
   not making much of a difference because too many starfish have
   washed up on shore. As the young man tosses another starfish into
   the water, he smiles and says, "It made a difference for that one."

Finally, remember to give praise when you see a child sharing or giving. Promote the concept of sharing (including non-material items as
well) as often as possible. Even if you needed to remind them of how
it felt when someone did not share, praise them anyway. Demonstrate
the joy of giving. You're setting an example and empowering them to
make the right choices as you explain how their act of giving made
someone else happy.

Inspire Giving

One of the best ways to teach children how to serve others is
through charitable giving. Volunteering is about giving, and there
are countless ways children can help others. With adult supervision, even young children can serve food at shelters or assist
adults when they deliver meals to the elderly. They can help plant
flowers at the school or community center. You could even get
them involved in a cleanup day in their neighborhood. To gain a
larger sense of community and serving, you could partner with
nationwide projects, like the one supported by National CleanUp
Day (www.nationalcleanupday.org). There are many outdoor

activities that teach children the importance of giving back to Mother Earth. Your local parks and recreations department may also have some volunteer opportunities for young children.

Simple painting activities can also teach children about sharing. Start by placing the children in groups of two; ask the children to decide on a subject and then color or paint that thing together. Affirm and celebrate this sharing experience with verbal praise throughout the activity.

Competitive hot-potato-style games are another great activity that supports giving. Sing the words to a song or play a song for the children while they pass a ball from one child to the next. In this game, no one wants to keep the ball for themselves in fear of becoming It!

Give one of the children in the classroom a handful of crackers or cookies to share. Allow the child to give one to each person in the room. This activity normalizes giving and helps young children understand that sharing is a regular part of everyday life. Children love this activity, and it encourages them to continue the act of giving at home. For instance, it may encourage them to offer family members part of their meal or even a special treat that they enjoy.

"I go" then "you go." Giving can be promoted, trained, and learned if practiced consistently. If a child leaves a toy in an open area, make sure they understand that it's up for grabs and others are allowed to play with it. Make it clear that if a child invites someone to play with them, they are also inviting them to play with their toys. If a child doesn't want another child to use their toy, either put that special toy away or set a timer so they can take turns playing with it. Let the child know that they will get ten minutes, and when the timer goes off, it's their friend's turn. This will demonstrate how taking turns can work, and it's not permanent.

Reflections

☼ What inspires you to give?

☼ How do you feel when you give to others?

☼ Educators give in so many ways; which are your favorites?

☼ Where do you go to find inspiration?

☼ Can you recall the last time you were inspired? Who inspired you? If you could thank that person, what would you say to them?

☼ What kinds of encouragement often inspire you?

☼ What kinds of encouragement do you give your students?

☼ How do you feel when your students or children give you something to thank you?

☼ Do you encourage random acts of giving?

3 Building Confidence: I Can't

ALTHOUGH I CONSIDER MYSELF to be a resilient person, there have been times when I have given up. Sometimes it took me a while to find my focus again, but I always kept trying. A great example of this was when I was trying to pass my teaching-credential exams. I remember how I felt after taking the exam a second time. Retrieving the mail and opening up that test score was devastating, or so I thought at the time. I had passed the math and oral portions of the exam but not the writing portion. Each time I took the test, I felt good about it when I left. On both occasions, I would receive the results weeks later and wonder why and how this was happening. Looking back I was pretty dramatic about the whole thing. My "why" was so comedic and drawn out it resembled the cry of a vaudeville stage actor.

I felt defeated for days. Eventually I took the test again and passed on my third attempt. How did I find the strength to persevere? It was right around this time in my life, in my twenties, that I strengthened my resolve by adapting to failure and redefining its purpose in my life. Looking back it seems like such a simple choice to make, but during my childhood and young-adult life, I felt as if I failed often, and it made me miserable. Things like striking out with the bases loaded during a baseball game or not being asked to dance at my high school Sadie Hawkins party were devastating at the time. If I had only known earlier, even five or six years ago, what I know now. No one ever showed me it was possible to accept failure, learn from it, and move on. Failure was simply not an option.

After I shifted my mindset about failure, my life changed for the better. I do not know whether my shifted mindset came as a result of listening to success stories or the wisdom of someone who knew how to channel my frustrations. I will probably never know exactly what inspired this shift. I do know that I am forever grateful for the impact it has had on my life. I know now that mistakes are simply learned lessons. I'm still standing today due to the countless times I have failed, wallowed a bit, repurposed the event, and tried again. My newfound perseverance has shown me that I am capable of anything and that I should never give up. I urge each of us to pass this mindset on to the children in our lives.

Throughout my teaching years, especially the years I spent with elementary-age children, there has been one phrase that I have heard over and over again: "I can't." In urban settings, it's quite popular to use this phrase in response to something stupid or funny on social media, and you may hear it exchanged in a group of friends. In the classroom, however, these two words have a very different meaning.

"I can't" language, along with a giving-up mentality, was a recurring theme with children whether I was in a program with three-year-olds or six-year-olds. I knew much of the sentiment they expressed derived from a lack of confidence and self-esteem. There is always a strong parallel between how a child feels about themselves and how they act. Thus, if we raise a confident child who grows up with healthy self-esteem and self-worth, they will have a basic understanding of their strengths and weaknesses. This basic understanding will allow a child to build on their strengths and strengthen their weaknesses. These children may be more inclined to keep trying instead of simply saying "I can't." So how can we, as adults, help a child reach a high level of confidence?

Parents are most likely the main influence on a child's sense of self-worth. Beginning as early as infancy, how a parent responds to their child contributes to their child's sense of self-worth. When a child feels worthy and valued by their parents, their confidence and self-esteem increase. When a child looks in the mirror and likes the person they see, a sense of self-worth has been fully established. Too often when there's a lack of self-worth, a child will exhibit behavioral problems at home or at school. How a child values themselves as a person not only affects family life and their performance at school, but it also impacts virtually all their relationships.

I tried to keep all this in mind in the frustrating moments when students would proclaim, "Mr. Haggood, I can't do that!" Because I was working primarily with young children, I made it a point to remember that they develop differently and at different rates. I successfully held my expectations at bay and let my students progress at their own pace. Praise and patience went hand in hand as I attempted to build my students' skills and self-esteem. From the onset of my teaching career, I was convinced that raising self-esteem in children was what I was good at. However, defeatist statements like "I can't learn my times tables," "I can't write very well," or "I can't draw at all" kept me puzzled for years. I couldn't seem to break those two words.

Everyone knows that accomplishing something can have a tremendously positive impact on your mood and your overall self-esteem, and failing to accomplish something can have a negative impact. I got so fed up with students starting a sentence with "I can't," I knew I had to try to do something about it. One day a brilliant idea came to me. The results were so positive that I continued to use this out-of-the-box teaching strategy every year of my teaching career.

The first thing I had to do was get the parents on board. I sent a permission letter to each family stating that my weeklong goal was to remove "I can't" from their child's vocabulary. The letter included the activities their child would be participating in, and it also explained how parents could support these activities at home. Once the parents returned the permission letters (and I undoubtedly answered one or two questions from curious parents), the weeklong objective began to take shape.

On Day 1, I told my students an "I can't" story from my own childhood. In an effort to draw them in and gain their interest, I massaged the truth of the story just a bit. The story began with me explaining that as the youngest boy of three brothers, I was always considered "the baby," and I hated it. My two brothers had succeeded in riding a bike without training wheels by their fourth birthday. I then told the students that when my own fourth birthday was approaching, it was my goal to ride my bike without training wheels. On the day of my fourth birthday, I was so excited and anxious to be like my brothers that I got on the bike and began to pedal, only to run smack into an ice cream truck. Laughs all around the room ensued. I emphasized my story's point by telling my students that it was at this moment that I started to doubt myself. I believed there would just be things in life that I couldn't do or be good at.

That Day 1 story set the stage for Day 2. For that day's activity, I asked the children to pull out a blank piece of paper. Each student folded their piece of paper in two, creating two columns (one on each side of the paper). While the students were doing this, I turned on soft music and carried out a guided-imagery technique that was supposed to help relax listeners. Then I reminded the students of my story from the previous day and asked them to close their eyes. I asked them to think about a time they wanted to try something new but didn't do it because they were afraid they would fail. I also encouraged each student to think of things they had already attempted unsuccessfully. The room's ambience created a focused environment for nonjudgmental and reflective thinking.

Once I had given the children time to think it over, I asked them to title the top left side of their paper "I CAN'T" all in caps. Next, I encouraged every child to list all the things they wished they could do or had the opportunity to do. When they finished their lists, I instructed them to label the opposite right column with "I CAN." I intentionally had the children leave that column blank. They then taped the unfinished lists to the top of their desks.

On Day 3 and Day 4, I asked the students to share their frustrations and defeated notions of what they could not do (I CAN'T). The students shared all kinds of things they felt they could not do, from riding a bike to perfecting division. I wanted these two days to be cathartic for the children and to let them share their thoughts without passing judgment or interrupting. It wasn't that I wanted each student to overcome and succeed at what they weren't good at. No one is good at everything. However, for young children (probably up until fifth grade), this "I can't" mindset can become overwhelmingly sorrowful and self-prophesizing. It can even create a pattern of low self-worth if children choose to focus on what they can't do. At this young age, important developmental milestones are happening, such as clarifying language and discovering algebraic concepts, but social identifiers really set the tone for young children.

On Day 5, each student was asked to wear black, no other colors. Because parents had already received my lesson plan and given me their approval and support, they anticipated this request. I had not shared my plan with anyone else. Of course onlookers from other classrooms wanted to know what was happening as our class lined up that morning. Teachers and students alike were curious about what Mr. Haggood and Room 30 were up to. I ignored the stares and led my students into the classroom. As we entered, I dramatically proclaimed, "Welcome Room 30, to the funeral of 'I CAN'T.'" Music filled the room as I played a prerecorded tape with ancestral drums beating. One or two of the students were asked to grab some drums and play along to add more flair to the moment. The classroom was rich with laughter as the students began to understand that a fun, lighthearted exercise was about to begin.

I asked the students to go to their desks and get the piece of paper they had written on Day 2. I told them to tear the paper or cut it in half, leaving the "I CAN" portion of the paper on their desk and holding on to the "I CAN'T" half. With a dramatic and commanding voice, I instructed them each to line up before we marched outside. As we marched, one or two students continued playing their drums.

I led my class to the green, forested portion of our campus. I had intentionally planned this exercise during a time when other classes were not outside. If our activity attracted the attention of other students and teachers, it would not be as effective. To gain full participation from my class, I had to make sure they were not distracted or subjected to judgmental stares or responses from their peers. I had timed everything perfectly and had my students' full attention.

With the drums still beating and a shovel in hand, I began to dig a small hole in the dirt. (I had received prior permission from the principal.) When the hole was dug, I asked each child to ball up their "I CAN'T" papers in their fist and toss them in the hole. I told them we were going to bury the phrase "I can't" so it would never be heard coming out of their mouths again. It was in this moment that I took the opportunity to deepen their understanding. When each student gathered around the hole, I withdrew from the lighthearted playacting and seriously spoke to my students:

"You have a choice. It may not seem like you have one at the moment when you are discouraged or your feelings are hurt, but you do have a choice. Your ability to love yourself and focus on your positive qualities will determine your station and status in life. The difference between low self-esteem and high self-esteem will be the difference between misery and happiness, between failure and success, between tears and laughter. Lastly, if you are unable to respect yourself, then don't expect others to do so. A greater self-esteem is the key to a better life."

This lighthearted and symbolically driven activity had transformed from a funny moment into a ceremony of renewal and celebration. The children and I marched back to class for the last portion of this social-emotional lesson.

Once all the students were back in the classroom and seated, they returned their focus to the "I CAN" portion of the paper that still remained on their desks. This last visual reminded the students of the weeklong lesson illustrating each portion of the process and their participation in it. After giving the children time to fill in their "I CAN" column, I gave them the opportunity to brag about all the wonderful things they could do. The lists were longer and more awesome as each child read theirs aloud to the class.

The week's activities had all built up to this. Each student's individual "I CAN" moments were praised by the class, whether they were sharing things they could already do or things they would be willing to try. I immediately noticed a change in my class. The children were celebratory, positive, and proud.

I saw the effect this experience had on my students and asked them to keep their lists. As the year went on, this activity continued to reinforce and motivate the children as they noted their future achievements on the "I CAN" list.

Although you will need to tread delicately with this project to ensure that you do not disrespect any burial rituals of the community you inherit as a teacher, assure the families that this exercise is a celebration of renewal. The payoff will be worth it when they see their child exhibit an observable increase in self-esteem! To this day, when I see students who have experienced this learning exercise, they still ask, "Is my paper still buried at the school?" In reply I ask, "What does that mean if it is still there?" I smile with pride as they say, "'I can't' is dead."

There are many takeaways from this experiment. Always dole out plenty of love. Teachers and parents who praise guessing and risk-taking show children that failure is an option and is not the end of the world. If a child fails at something or shows no skill at a particular talent, praise the effort but don't unrealistically praise the results. This reaffirms within a child that it is okay to not perform perfectly at everything. Resilience is a much-undervalued character trait in our children. We can teach resilience by emphasizing that mistakes are lessons learned, which demystifies the importance of the event and decreases feelings of failure or disappointment. Model getting back up on your feet after a disappointment; this real-life example of perseverance will reinforce this idea for children.

When I was a child, I was saturated with warm compliments. My parents were praisers. It's as if they belonged to a Parent Praise Club that met weekly. Conversely my parents only needed to make eye contact with me when they weren't happy with my behavior. Words were not necessary; a disapproving look was usually all that was needed to alter and correct my steps. However, as I shared at the beginning of this chapter, I felt as though I failed often because no one taught me that it was okay to not be good at everything. It took me many years to build my resilience, and I can't help but wonder how this "I can't" experiment would have affected me as a child.

I always take everything I have learned and use it to reflect on my own practice as a parent. I parent using an 80/20 rule. When I reflect on any given day or week, I should be sharing positive words 80 percent of the time and using a negative tone only 20 percent of the time. This four-to-one ratio ensures that I am spending the majority of my time building up my child instead of knocking them down. Focusing on positive language will result in more "I can" statements and decrease the frequency of "I can't." This has proven effective for me and my children. It's important for parents to remember that no one wants to hear all the things they are doing wrong all the time.

The adage that a child will do what you do and not what you say is key as well. You may need to polish your own mirror to achieve lasting results in the self-image of a child. A child in your care will ultimately look to you as a mirror of their feelings. If you are negative all the time, the child will be too. At least in part, children develop their self-image from your reactions.

Although each child is different, there are many universal tools that promote building confidence. A child's confidence stems from adult praise, especially in response to their achievements and accomplishments. When you praise a child, they will think well of themselves. It does not matter whether this praise comes from family, friends, or educators. As children learn new skills and develop new goals, they will reach greater milestones, especially in their social-emotional development. Remember that feeling good about what you *can* do and not focusing on what you *can't* do is important. This is a key to being successful at any age.

You Can Do It

Stacking blocks not only helps young children develop hand-eye coordination. If you join in the activity, you are showing an interest in the child and what they are doing. According to Dr. William Sears, a renowned pediatrician and author of several parenting books, adults should join children in playtime activities because it fosters a child's sense of self-worth and confidence (Sears, accessed 2018). Whether you are the aide on the playground or the parent in the backyard or living room, you are not wasting your time when you participate in simple activities.

Setting the table makes a child feel useful and successful. When a child is proud of their ability and skill, they will continue to feel confident. The element of play will be useful in this activity, as children will soon be asking you if they can set the table.

Another activity that child educators encourage is gardening. This can be done at home or at school. Whether it's starting a garden by planting a new flower or vegetable or partaking in an existing garden, children will delight at the opportunity to watch the process of growth. Just as students are growing themselves, educators and parents can enhance their learning and confidence by elaborating on the growth process.

Tidying up the classroom area or a child's room is a great activity for building confidence. Educators should encourage children consistently to build organizational skills beneficial to later living. Taking ownership of their room environment, clothing materials, and personal hygiene are all connected benefits of this teaching. Educators and parents who emphasize ownership may hear the benefits of their encouragement as a child says, "I need to clean up my area before I go outside."

Involving a child in an activity in their local community will increase confidence. Whether it's a recreational activity or music lessons, children thrive when they are building a skill. Sports teams allow children to feel like part of a larger effort, and they will gain social-emotional value from taking turns and accepting outcomes. Solo activities increase independence and foster developmental gains.

Reflections

☼ What do you do when you want to give up?

☼ What can you say or do when someone around you wants to give up?

☼ What does feeling defeated mean to you?

☼ What did your parents do to uplift you? What did they do that weakened your self-image?

☼ How do you handle negative feedback?

☼ How do you get someone to try something they believe they cannot do?

☼ Has anyone ever given you a second chance?

☼ How did it feel when someone didn't give up on you?

☼ What makes you feel confident?

☼ What image do you reflect to children?

4 Empathy and Compassion: Christof Johnson

OVER THE PAST FEW DECADES, much has been said and written about the poor academic achievement among students in urban settings. Many children and their families are living with severe economic disadvantage. I can bear witness to the challenges of helping children who face risk factors such as poverty, homelessness, and neighborhoods characterized by crime, violence, and drugs, and sociocultural factors such as discrimination, racial barriers, and language barriers. It can be overwhelming.

Although dealing with crime and feelings of despair is a constant battle for many folks in my district, I feel honored and privileged to work where I do. Why? Probably because I love the feeling of being needed. From the moment I stepped on my campus, I knew I needed this community, and I knew they could benefit from what I had to offer.

I remember a particular incident as if it were just yesterday. It was the spring of 1994, early on in my career, and I was teaching third grade. It was around 2:15 in the afternoon, and my class and I were enjoying a game of kickball for our physical education portion of the day. As I participated with my class (something I always did), I noticed that two of my students, Cassandra and Nicki, had wandered over near the fence.

The fence ran parallel to the heavy traffic of Vernon Avenue, a busy Los Angeles street in an urban neighborhood. Truthfully this area hadn't really recovered since the Rodney King uprising in 1991. Just one block away, Los Angeles police officers had pulled Rodney King from his vehicle and brutally beat him. Following the incident, there was an investigation into the controversial event. Every Los Angeles police officer that was indicted was pronounced not guilty. On the day of the court ruling, thousands of Los Angeles residents took to the streets in protests that escalated into physical violence and the destruction of buildings, stores, and cars. This tragic event was not only economically devastating to our community, but it also deepened the racial and socioeconomic divide in the city.

I quickly left the game and jogged toward Cassandra and Nicki. I noticed the girls were speaking with a woman who was on the opposite side of the fence. I walked over and asked, "Girls, what's going on?"

Cassandra replied, "This is Christof's mom."

Christof was one of the students in my class.

On the other side of the fence, I saw a woman who, although older, mirrored Christof with her beautifully dark, chiseled face. With a frail voice, the woman spoke. "I'm sorry, Teacher. I just wanted to see my boy."

From the look in her eyes, I knew that this was a precious and sensitive moment. She began to cry and said, "There he is!"

At that moment, I noticed the grocery cart she had with her. It was filled with miscellaneous items. I knew then that she was homeless and possibly on drugs.

I looked back at my class and saw that they, including Christof, were still engaged in kickball and oblivious to what was going on at the gate.

Choked up by the moment, I invited her to come over to our side of the fence. She looked embarrassed and began to walk away.

I called out, "Ms. Johnson, Ms. Johnson, come back."

She didn't come back. Instead, she waved goodbye and said, "I'll be back."

As I turned to glance at my students, I noticed that Nicki had already gone over to Christof, about fifty yards away, presumably to tell him that his mother had come to see him. Christof looked shocked and humiliated. He took off running across the playground toward the boys' bathroom. I yelled for him to come back, but he continued running as fast as he could.

I asked my class to line up before I went into the bathroom to console Christof. It was dark inside the bathroom even though it was sunny outside—an unnerving example of how inner-city schools function. Christof had his head down with a wet towel over his face. He was crying profusely. I hugged him and urged him to come out of the bathroom and rejoin the class. As we exited the bathroom, the whole class stared at Christof. Undoubtedly Nicki had told all of them the entire chain of events.

The class was quiet as we walked up the stairs to our Room 30 classroom. I had my arms around Christof, who was still weeping, and tried to keep it together. My mind raced because we were ten minutes away from the end of the school day. That left only enough time for dismissal, which meant I needed to issue homework so the children could grab their things and go home. On the other hand, I felt like I needed to address what had happened. What should I do?

I decided I would use this moment to honor this young black boy. My heart raced, and I allowed all the students to go inside except for Christof. We stayed outside on the second-floor walkway in front of our classroom.

As I glanced through the classroom window, I could see the students pretending to grab jackets, books, and personal belongings in anticipation of going home. They were anxious and interested in the discussion that Christof and I were about to have. I knew that a class dialogue had likely begun inside. Their homework was not yet issued, which was very out of the ordinary. Routine and redundancy was a teaching strategy that I followed like brushing my teeth each morning. The students could tell that I was prioritizing this moment with Christof.

"How you feeling, Christof?" I asked to ease the moment.

Eyes welled with tears and his voice barely audible, Christof said, "I hate her. Coming to this school where she know I got friends. I'll never hear the end of this. Man, why she come here?"

More tears ensued, and the children began to line up inside for dismissal. I realized that this must be a nightmare for Christof. All of this young boys' friends would soon know—if they didn't know already—that Christof's mother was homeless, a sure embarrassment for any little boy in the hood. Judgment, humiliation, and embarrassment seemed to be the expected outcome for Christof at that moment. I asked Christof to stay after school so we could continue our conversation. He agreed as I began to open the door.

With a single-file line almost completed, the door now swung all the way open. I heard Gary shout out, "It's okay, Christof, my cousin is on drugs."

Then Destiny yelled out, "Yeah, Christof, it's cool. My dad ain't never home."

Yolanda chimed in, "My sister gambles, and she lost all her money."

Jerletha literally squealed, "That's nothing, my brother still pees in his bed and he fifteen."

My students were empathizing with Christof and lending him support in this most precious moment. I was proud—proud that I had fostered not just a learning environment but a familial environment with caring and positive temperaments. As Christof stood outside the door, I witnessed a touching ceremony where the girls and boys in my class lined up to give Christof hugs and handshakes. Christof's face turned from embarrassment to surprise at the empathy and compassion of his classmates. I, too, was astonished at the maturity of such young students. This offer of empathy was amazing to me and supported my mission to always get to know my students first!

The payoff is huge for educators and parents who take time to develop a child's empathy. It can make all the difference. Children are less likely to hurt and more likely to help someone if they can imagine themselves in that person's place and can share that person's thoughts and feelings. Early childhood educators can teach young children to empathize with others by helping them learn and practice empathy in direct connection with bullying situations. They can help young children understand how children who are bullied might feel and how they themselves would feel if they were the recipients of such taunting. They can prepare children to become helpful bystanders by helping them recognize when a child who is bullied is feeling hurt and how they might help that child feel better.

Children learn empathy from watching us. We develop trust and secure attachments with them when we empathize with them. Because they want to emulate us, they will build empathy for others. They pay close attention to how you treat your coworkers, neighbors, family members, or the waitress who served your dinner, and the way you treat others sets the example for the children in your care. Your views on other cultures and types of people will resonate with them. Expressing interest in people from other backgrounds, whether it's in the classroom or at home, is demonstrating empathy for others. Reasoning how different their lives may be allows a child to walk in someone else's shoes if even for a moment.

Christof and his amazing resilience and courage will always remind me of that. The way his smile returned following this incident and his sense of relief was amazing to see. Initially, any child who has experienced trauma or unfortunate circumstances would deflate and

feel humiliated. Watching Christof regain his confidence and inno-
cence was incredible. When Christof returned to the playground and
reclaimed his "king of kickball" status was when I knew we had him
back.

Christof's relationship with his mother may have been an emotional one, but my students made it just a little bit easier to digest
when they showed empathy that day.

Promoting Compassion

You can help young children understand how children who are
bullied might feel and how they themselves would feel if they
were the recipients of such taunting. It's important to recognize
that even young children may demonstrate this behavior by
making mean faces at other children or refusing to play with
someone. You can prepare children to become helpful bystanders
by helping them recognize what bullying is, how it hurts the child
who is being teased or bullied, and how they might help that
child feel better.

Showing a video of the consequences of bullying is a great way
to introduce the impact of their bullying and teasing. The video
must be developmentally appropriate and should contain the
possible effects for an individual who is constantly tormented
with verbal or physical abuse from others. Promoting compassion
with the visual representation of a video might allow for more
heartfelt empathy than just auditory repetitive responses.

Create dialogues with children who can begin to empathize
with others by first examining their own feelings. Use visual
representations like pictures from magazines that show children
from many different races, cultures, and backgrounds. Introduce
simple activities like sorting objects by their differences and then

working with the children to develop an appreciation for the differences in each of us.

Explain how an act of kindness can bring a smile to someone and help them have a better day. Discuss how an act of kindness is the opposite of bullying because it gives a person a good feeling rather than taking away a good feeling. Ask children to describe one nice thing they did for someone else, how it made the other person feel, and how it made them feel. Have each child plan one act of kindness that he or she will do that day for someone else, whether that person is a classmate or a family member.

To help teach children about empathy, have them participate in a "Labeling Feelings" activity. Ask them to draw, discuss, or role-play how they might feel if they were being bullied or saw someone being bullied and how they would feel if they were bullying someone else.

Reflections

☼ What can you do to teach empathy in others?

☼ When was the last time you empathized with someone else?

☼ How have others supported your feelings?

☼ What is helpful to do when others feel a sense of shame?

☼ What social problems are you facing in your surrounding community?

☼ What steps have you taken to provide the children in your care with a safe and respectful environment?

☼ How do you help children respect and appreciate diversity?

☼ How do you help children understand bullying behavior?

☼ Have you ever participated in a random act of kindness? What did you do?

☼ What are some ways to demonstrate a random act of kindness?

Gender Stereotyping: Dolls and Trains

EDUCATORS MUST WORK TOWARD HAVING a welcoming classroom environment. This means being tolerant of the various viewpoints, opinions, and upbringings of students and parents. It can be a struggle for educators to foster tolerance, especially when an issue is considered controversial by some parents. One example of this is the discussion around gender norms. Because these notions are typically influenced by a person's culture, many parents have strong opinions on how boys and girls are expected to behave.

In many societies, girls are often stereotyped as the caregiver. In some cultures, girls are expected to be nurturing and caring, and they are expected to take care of the house. Although this is changing, stereotypes still exist today. In my day, this stereotype was evident at an early age. I witnessed counselors enroll females in electives like home economics or sewing as I was enrolled in woodshop or technology. The stereotyping of both genders must stop in educational communities if we plan to have a society where children are free to explore all their gifts, talents, and options.

Thankfully our society has seen the need to invest in girls understanding their power. We have done this in many avenues, including amending the Constitution and encouraging all school subjects. The constitutional amendment is called Title IX of the Education Amendments of 1972, which stipulates that any educational program or activity that receives federal funding cannot discriminate on the basis of sex. Its implications are many; recently, for example, Title IX has been the basis of complaints against schools charged with not properly responding to the issue of sexual assault. Its most famous impact has been on school sports programs, and the impact of the amendment is still being felt today. According to the National Collegiate Athletic Association (NCAA), in the 2015–16 academic year, 211,886 women participated in college sports in the United States, representing a 25 percent increase over the previous decade.

There is also a push for more female employees in science, technology, engineering, and math careers. In the past few years, there has been a plethora of STEM/STEAM-oriented toys and activities designed to help girls and boys develop an interest in science, technology, engineering, art, and mathematics. As a society, we understand that girls are underrepresented academically in the sciences not because they're not good at the subjects or uninterested in them, but because they're guided away from them, both implicitly and explicitly. With the advent and marketing of STEM/STEAM toys, our society is trying to do better. The liberation of one gender finally has some momentum.

Although progress has been made against gender stereotyping, it's important to realize we live in a complex society where some still believe that boys should never cry and that girls should not express their anger. For many boys, the normal emotion of "sad," which might induce tears, is replaced by being "mad." And many girls suppress their emotions in fear of being labeled an unflattering name. I often hear parents (usually fathers) of preschool boys shaming their sons for crying. Unfortunately some people in our society seem to have outlawed boys crying if they are over the age of eight. This warped normality troubles me and always has.

If it's true that we as a society are attempting to build gender equality, I suggest that we need to address the social-emotional impact needed for boys. Otherwise our attempts at gender equality may be inadequate. Remembering that boys also face gender-based challenges is important. Many believe that boys are just more impulsive than girls, that they lack patience and have a harder time sitting and waiting for longer periods of time. Therefore, when boys can't sit and wait and they are disruptive, admonishment, shame, and anger may result. Leading psychologists and researchers Michael Thompson and Dan Kindlon, coauthors of *Raising Cain: Protecting the Emotional Life of Boys*, suggest that allowing our boys to understand their emotional language and honor their vulnerability are essential components in celebrating and protecting the emotional life of boys (2000).

We should challenge boys and allow them to develop skills as well. Dr. Thompson says, "You throw boys as a group in to a very challenging situation and let them figure it out and find their own leadership." These boys will gain a lot of confidence. Whether mowing a lawn, making a sandwich, or retrieving the daily mail, boys need responsibilities and skills. Life lessons are approaching the three-year-old preschool boy, and it is up to us to prepare him.

We seem to still believe that although most boys are interested in becoming dads someday, there really is no need for them to practice parenting skills. This is strange because, as a society, we seem to publicize and realize the pressure put on a father to raise a boy into a man. Sons see their fathers as role models. A son's relationship—or lack thereof—with his father greatly influences how he feels about fatherhood. My father was sensitive enough, but he possessed the same "macho man" attitude that many fathers have. It was not his personality that influenced me the most, however—it was his absence. He was missing for the majority of my young life, which is the case for many children across the United States.

In a 2012 finding by the US Census Bureau, it was estimated that 57.6 percent of black children, 31.2 percent of Hispanic children, and 20.7 percent of white children have absent biological fathers. This raises an important question: what are we as a society doing to promote fatherhood and ensure that men embrace fatherhood? Why do so many men run from the possibility of being a dad? The question of why men run from their responsibilities cannot be answered with a simple explanation. Some may say that men are genetically insensitive and are repeating cycles of generations of men who abandon their children. I suggest that our culture has perpetuated these stereotypes by not providing adequate training for boys to become men and fathers and by encouraging boys to suppress emotion.

My hope is that our society will continue to provide equal opportunities for boys and girls. I believe that allowing boys and girls to share a wide range of emotions is normal and fosters healthy child development. I decided to become an advocate for a gender-neutral classroom. With that intention, I decided to explore the real-life gap between the social conditioning of girls and boys by introducing dolls in my preschool classroom.

Preschool professionals know that from cognitive and motor development to social-emotional growth, no other single toy comes close to the impact that dolls can have. Interacting with baby dolls not only gives boys and girls an opportunity to develop nurturing skills for parenting, but it encourages them to be loving to others. I was surprised to learn the multitude of ways that dolls and care play can positively impact children as they grow.

Before I could fully embrace my gender-neutral classroom, I sought to gain parent understanding and permission. I often do this with anything risky because I don't want parents to be unpleasantly surprised by any changes in my classroom, although preschool educators typically don't face issues this controversial. I decided to mail each family a letter explaining my decision to have a gender-neutral classroom and told them that I would be encouraging boys and girls alike to play with baby dolls. The letter was mailed home on a Monday, and by the end of the week, I had seven parents inquiring why this was being done. Of the seven, three were dads, and I knew they would be the hardest to convince that this would benefit their child.

I decided to meet with the moms separately because I suspected that each gender would have slightly different perspectives and objections moving forward. I was right. When I conveyed my intention—having their sons experience what it might be like to become a father—it was all they needed to hear. The fathers, on the other hand, were not so easy to persuade. They were skeptical that giving the boys dolls would somehow benefit them. Their concerns were much more relevant to sexist social conditioning; they assumed playing with dolls would soften their boys or lead to bullying. Once I assured them that the boys would be handling the baby dolls only within the confines of the classroom, the bullying argument went out the window.

There were still two fathers in particular who seemed to be disgusted by the whole idea. They viewed boys interacting with baby dolls as a "sissy" thing, and since their boys were growing up in the hood, they were not okay with the idea at all. Tough environments pose additional challenges for boys and girls. Boys are encouraged to overemphasize aggressive behavior. Simple behavioral norms like walking and talking are often manipulated to exhibit toughness. It can be perceived as a sign of weakness for boys to show emotion such as crying or whining. These two men presumably thought it would damage their sons' masculinity to play with baby dolls.

I decided to share the same affirming intentions that I shared with the mothers previously. I argued that these boys would someday be better fathers and better men because they participated in nurturing and caring behaviors around a doll. This fell on deaf ears.

A separate meeting was set up with these two men, Mr. Oliver and Mr. Meeks. I knew that I would have to bring more heat (evidence) to this conference for their boys to be allowed to participate. First I assured them that I was only adding to their character. Opportunities to interact with planes, trains, and automobiles would also be present. Even if I put a doll in the hand of every boy in my classroom, odds are they still may prefer matchbox cars and trucks. Little boys adore anything that flies, sails, drives, digs, or mixes. The groundwork was laid, and the fathers realized that adding a doll to their sons' lives would not alter their masculinity; it would only encourage their human development.

Mr. Oliver and Mr. Meeks were invited to see their boys interact with the dolls, and thankfully when observing, they received the message intended. Boys and girls need real-life opportunities to open up and engage in potential scenarios so they become more familiar. There was always pushback as I introduced this activity in subsequent classes. Year after year, I faced rolled eyes and negative language from other colleagues and parents not able to connect this strategy to the broader vision. However, this was not the case with the boys in my class. Initially most of the boys would behave stereotypically, as though some foreign invader had come into their class. However, creating an environment that promoted gender equity where boys were not pressured to "macho up" allowed all the children to relax and just have fun with the dolls.

It has been fulfilling to see the positive effects of my gender-neutral classroom. One incident that stands out to me is when one of my male former students returned to the school as a parent. He thanked me for the years of empowering him in my classroom and the mentoring years that followed, and he elaborated on raising a daughter and the impact his classroom experience of interacting with baby dolls had on his life. Ironically this interaction stood out to him most because at the time he considered it silly and laughable.

As boys age, there are fewer opportunities to talk with them about their future responsibilities. That is why it is so important that we allow boys to play around with potential scenarios at an early age so they can mature into responsible young men. Empowering boys as they become men is an issue facing the entire nation, and we must engage.

We, the collective "we" that includes parents, family, teachers, and society at large, teach our children how to live and love and have fun in this world. Let's stop denying boys access to dolls simply because they don't ask for them. We should work to introduce a range of toys to all children, to stop categorizing toys by gender, and to provide the material goods that will help all children develop the interests that might later drive their passions.

Should there be an expectation that school systems include gender-based strategies and activities into their curriculum? I say that we must.

Challenging Stereotypes

Ask children to stand up based on preferences within their developmental age. Who likes chocolate ice cream? Please stand. Who likes movies? Please stand. After naming several examples, have a conversation with children regarding how we form opinions and where they come from.

Explore differences with your children through visuals. Bring in several pictures and videos of different cultures and individuals and demonstrate for young students how diverse we all are.

Write a common stereotype based on gender, ethnicity, or social-economic status on a strip of paper. Examples could be, "Cheerleading is only for girls" or "Basketball is only for boys." Give each student one of these strips. Assist one student at a time as they read their strip's stereotype aloud. Then have them place the strip on a blown-up balloon. Ask the rest of the students to answer whether this stereotype is true for everyone. After the students debunk the stereotype, the child who was given that strip may burst the balloon it is attached to. (The balloon can be popped with a needle under adult supervision.) Repeat this sequence with each student.

Preschool-age children and other young children can have very defined ideas about gender roles, such as that certain tasks are for girls and others are for boys. Role-playing games help children identify stereotypes and realize that both boys and girls can be good at many things. Start this activity by having the teacher or leader read a story card where children are behaving stereotypically. Here is an example: "Kevin says that he will not let Tameka play soccer because she is a girl." Ask the children to discuss why these stereotypes are inaccurate and how they can avoid making assumptions about people when interacting with their peers.

Videos are powerful representations of how we form our stereotypes. Find various developmentally appropriate video footage of individuals who do not represent stereotypical norms, such as a black farmer, an Asian rapper, a female mechanic, and so forth. Follow the video with a discussion.

Reflections

☼ What are some of the ways you empower boys and girls?

☼ What are some activities that we as a society (and maybe even you) do not allow boys or girls to participate in?

☼ As a teacher, what measures have you taken to make sure boys and girls have the same opportunities?

☼ How do you praise the children in your care? Do boys and girls receive the same praise for the same behavior?

☼ Describe an incident of gender bias or stereotyping you've witnessed in your classroom.

☼ What are some of the consequences of gender imbalance in the classroom?

☼ How do you address the gender imbalance in children's literature?

☼ How do you handle sexist behavior in young children?

☼ Do you think that boys are typically more likely to get into trouble? Why?

☼ How might stereotypes affect people as they grow up? How did they affect you?

6
Body Image:
The Mirror Doesn't Tell All

WOMEN HAVE MADE ENORMOUS STRIDES in education, politics, and the workplace, but girls still struggle with body image beginning at increasingly younger ages. Girls' dissatisfaction centers particularly around weight and perceiving themselves as fat. This could lead to an eating disorder, which can be life threatening. A study conducted by the Agency for Healthcare Research and Quality showed that hospitalizations for eating disorders in children under twelve increased by 119 percent between 1999 and 2006 (2009). More recent numbers are unavailable, but experts believe the problem is getting worse. Poor body image affects up to 80 percent of women and girls and around 35 percent of men and boys (Gallivan 2014). It has been seen in children as young as five years old.

A child's image of themselves can often shape the rest of their life. I realized this early on and have always used this knowledge in my classroom. I was teaching students in the nineties, a time when society was not as concerned with promoting a girl's self-image as it is today. I took my responsibility as an educator very seriously. Some may think that children are not concerned about their body image and that they are too young to place emphasis on its importance. As early childhood educators can tell you, children are very aware of how their body looks, whether they are speaking with pride about the clothes they are wearing, showing you a scratch or boo-boo they just got, or bragging about how tall they are becoming. It is easy for adults to forget that children deal with body-image issues too, and being criticized or teased about your appearance can be hurtful at any age.

A person's perception of their reflection can be caused by mental, emotional, and physical factors, or a combination of any of the three. For instance, if seeing their reflection causes the viewer to become thoughtful, this is a mental reflection. An emotional reflection triggers one's feelings. A physical reflection stems from one's visual judgment of their appearance.

When I was in my eleventh year as an educator, I decided it was time to raise awareness and rebut the negative stereotype messages children receive about their bodies. The catalyst for this decision was Britney Piper. I met Britney when she entered my preschool classroom many years ago. To this day, I think of her as a combination of Pippi Longstocking and a modern-day Amazing Grace. Her mother enrolled her at four years of age, and she was eager to begin schooling. As I approached her on her first day, I asked Britney, "Are you ready to go to school?" Britney responded excitedly yes. Her mom, Brenda, told me that Britney couldn't wait to start school and make new friends.

Britney's days in preschool went by without incident. She was easily liked by the other girls and boys in class and was able to resolve conflicts on the playground between other students. Britney was athletic and had a radiant smile that would light up an auditorium. Students and adults alike often envied her height. Even at a young age, Britney towered over her classmates. She stood out even when she attempted to stay in the background.

However, when Britney was eight years old, Ms. Sezanne, Britney's teacher, confided in me that she was concerned. She stated that during breakfast and lunch, Britney was barely eating. When Ms. Sezanne urged Britney to eat, Britney either cried or attempted to eat very little. It was becoming a daily occurrence, and the teaching staff was worried. Initially when they questioned Britney about why she was not eating, she would just say she wasn't hungry.

Suspicion about Britney's aversion to food began when Britney stopped eating the district-supplied meals for breakfast or lunch. Instead she would nibble on an apple or another low-calorie snack from her backpack. Despite the urging of teaching staff, she would not only refuse to eat but would also bow her head in complete non-verbal resistance. This personality shift was very unlike the vibrant Britney everyone had come to know and love, and this upset the staff. When the staff brought the concern to her mom, she shrugged it off as something not to worry about because Britney did the same thing at home from time to time. This was not the helpful resolution the staff had hoped for.

After the disheartening moment with Britney's mom, Ms. Sezanne came to me. I listened as she told me the shocking reason why Britney barely ate. After many days of being questioned about her eating habits by the staff, Britney finally offered an explanation. She said her stepfather (who had never visited the school) had called her fat, and he told her that she was eating too much. When staff asked her if this was still occurring, she nodded and said that it was happening daily. What was perhaps most upsetting was that Britney's mom seemed to be aware of the verbal abuse Britney suffered, but she brushed it off as not important. Her mom's response to the verbal lashings was to send Britney to school with a healthy but meager calorie-controlled meal.

It is surprisingly common for children to be the victims of body shaming in their own homes. A fair amount of unhappiness and pressure also results from the media, which often presents images that portray a narrow standard of beauty. Although most girls and boys would rather see real photos of models and not the touched-up ones, they still seem to compare themselves to and continue to strive toward those unrealistic images. This has become a crisis in our country. Too many boys and girls feel they do not measure up in some way, whether in their looks, intellect, or social status. Since not all children come from a supportive home, educators must positively influence children in our schools.

With Britney in mind, I decided that we as a staff needed to intervene in a significant way. I wanted to make a difference not only for Britney, but also for others who may be going through similar issues. Although our curriculum at the time included a social-emotional component, the staff and I concluded that it was not specific enough. In its current state, it would not appropriately address necessary topics such as prejudice and body shaming.

We decided to take action by installing an activity called "The Beauty of Reflection" so that our students could start to appreciate their physical appearance. Several full-body mirrors were brought in and placed throughout our classrooms. To each mirror we attached prompts such as "I love my _____" and "I like the way my _____ look(s)." We used the mirror as a tool to enhance the confidence of our students with the hope that this activity would promote inner beauty as the purest form of beauty.

At first, of course, it took a while to get some of the children to even look in the mirror. Occasionally we would glance over and see a girl walk by but not stay too long. However, with the encouraging coaching and modeling of the adult staff in the room, the children finally warmed up to the mirror. It became a sort of experiment for the staff and a great evaluation and analysis of confidence.

To our surprise, some students whom we thought of as confident were not at all. A child we thought had major confidence because of her extensive language and leadership skills froze in front of the mirror and could not point out one thing she liked about herself. In moments like this, the staff and I had to get creative.

Although the children may not have noticed it, this activity ran much deeper than just the sentence prompts. When a student stood in front of the mirror, we would urge them to practice standing upright for great posture, all the while saying "please," "thank you," and other kind phrases. We hoped to subtly teach our students to exhibit good manners and practice being generous for the sole purpose of making someone else happy. We also encouraged them to look at themselves in the mirror and laugh. This helped the viewer lighten up and loosen the stoic expression we tend to have when examining ourselves in the mirror. These simple activities and interactions allowed students to become comfortable with looking in the mirror.

Within weeks of introducing the mirror activity, we could see a real difference. Girls who at first would "meet and greet" with the mirror but not speak had become much more confident about their appearance. "I love my eyes" or "I like the way my curls look," they would proclaim. We even saw a marked difference in Britney's confidence levels. This activity and classroom experiment also taught me that confident students make better learners.

Although this activity was originally developed with girls in mind, I have come to realize that boys benefit from it as well. This is a great activity for boys who see themselves as awkward or believe that their physical bodies have let them down (yes, boys have these thoughts even at a young age). It can build their self-confidence too.

Children are still learning how to address and process their feelings, so with an exercise like this you will have tears at first. Like any good teachable moment, encouragement and positive coaching is needed. The end goal is for every child in the classroom to appreciate their beauty. Use your position as an educator to inspire boys and girls. Here is an example of an age-appropriate lesson on self-image:

I am the only ME I've got, and I am unique. There are two major parts of ME. There is the inside ME and the outside ME. The outside ME is what you see: the way I act, the image I portray, the way I look, and the things I do. The outside ME is very important. It is my messenger to the world, and much of my outside ME is what communicates with you. I value what I have done, the way I look, and what I share with you.

With small children, remind them that their body is changing. Stay aware of messages they may be receiving from TV and other media that do not promote positive body image and have conversations with the child about it. Be an example to the child by exhibiting a strong positive attitude about your own body. Remember, when you express feelings about your body or going on a diet, listening ears are near. The power is yours! Shape the message you want the child to hear; the brain mirrors what it is exposed to. Move away from making disparaging remarks about your body image. Do not make negative comments about the way other people look either. This sends a contradictory message to an impressionable child.

Looks become increasingly important in adolescence, and this causes body-image issues to spike, but positive experiences during a person's early childhood can influence how they handle their body image years later. Children do not become thirteen overnight. Over the course of many years, educators can set the stage for a healthy body image and outlook.

An educator's goal is to help children feel comfortable in their own skin. But, more importantly, educators must help children learn that it's not what's on the outside that's most important, it's what's on the inside. When a child learns how to look inward, they will get to know themselves better, and they will discover all the wonderful things about themselves that can't be seen in their reflection. Imagine a classroom where each child realizes that every person on the planet is imperfect, flawed, and beautiful. Hallelujah!

Promoting Healthy Behaviors

Ask the children to write down three or four things they like about themselves. If you are working with very young children, have them sit in a circle and share these things aloud instead. Once you have heard their answers, talk about how each of these things makes them special and unique. Assure them that it's okay to like themselves.

Put full-length mirrors throughout your classroom and/or home with positive prompts taped to them. Encourage the children to admire their reflections.

Create a physical-health gratitude book so children can continue to develop healthy habits as they appreciate their physical health. The book may include physical activities for the children to participate in or a record of the healthy foods they have been eating.

Many songs about accepting others and yourself are available for preschool through K–5 grade levels. Play these songs and allow the children to dance and sing along. By listening to songs with these types of messages, children gain insight and awareness of their similarities and differences.

Ask your students to make a self-esteem collage. They will delight at the opportunity to self-define. Give each student a large piece of poster board and a stack of magazines to go through, then have them browse the pages to find pictures that represent themselves and their talents, abilities, and aspirations. This particular exercise will remind them what a valuable individual they are. If a student kept their collage and displayed it somewhere they would see it often, like in their bedroom, imagine the long-lasting positive effects this could have.

Have your classroom watch as you make a self-esteem bucket. Take a plastic bucket and hammer several nails into its bottom. Explain to the students that the nails represent hurtful comments or life experiences that could lead to a negative self-image. Fill the bucket with water; the water represents a child's self-esteem. Now start removing the nails and watch how the water drains out of the bucket. Use this demonstration to spark discussion. Then work with each student to brainstorm ways to "plug the holes" and increase self-esteem.

Reflections

☼ How do you define a healthy body image?

☼ Why is a healthy body image important?

☼ What process do you have in place to help children develop a healthy body image?

☼ What are the signs of an eating disorder in a young child?

☼ How can you tell if a child is just going through a phase or if it's something more?

☼ What makes a difference in the way you support girls versus boys?

☼ Who are the confident men and women in your life? Where did they get their confidence from?

☼ What are the ways you affirm yourself?

☼ What are three positive traits about yourself? Why do you consider them positive?

☼ What is the one thing about yourself that is most difficult to accept? Why?

7

Home Culture:
The Godmother

In my third year of teaching, I had gotten into a groove with my instruction and classroom management. The way I engaged with my students was becoming recognized by the school community. Staff and parents alike were beginning to speak of my classroom techniques and inspirational activities.

It was also during my third year of teaching that I met a family that would change my life. It was a normal school day, and I was headed toward my classroom, Room 30. As I approached Room 28, I noticed a boy sitting outside the door, dejected. I was concerned for two reasons. One, the ground was very dirty, and two, his head was down, which conflicted with the uplifting spirit I tried to share with everyone. I asked who he was and why he was sitting there and learned that his name was Tyler. He was on time-out, a strategy all too familiar in the day. What was unusual about the situation was that Tyler had been placed on time-out outdoors.

I gathered my thoughts before knocking on Mr. Andrews's door. I was flabbergasted that a teacher would leave a student outside their classroom. The student on time-out could hurt themselves, leave and go home, or go to the office and report that they were left outside. In all of these situations, the teacher could lose their job. When I questioned Mr. Andrews's time-out approach, I strategized by telling him that I was simply looking out for him. That tactic worked, because after speaking with him, Tyler was admitted back into the classroom.

The next day, I spoke with Ms. Awap, another faculty member, who provided the insight I needed to understand Mr. Andrews's method of behavior modification. Ms. Awap informed me that Mr. Andrews was a deposed corporate worker who decided that he would try teaching in the city because it would pay more and require less from him. She also informed me that many teachers were opting for teaching positions in the inner city because they were getting what she called "combat pay" for teaching in urban areas. Combat pay? I was outraged and insulted. I decided that by example I was going to educate an army of students that would surpass all stereotypical expectations. My students would be my weapons.

What I didn't expect was for change to begin the very next day. As I was outside my door watching my students enter my classroom the next morning, I saw Yolanda Anderson, Tyler's mother. Walking heavily like Sofia (Oprah) from *The Color Purple*, who uttered the movie's most classic line, "Get my babies outta here," Yolanda was approaching, and she had Tyler by the arm behind her.

"Good morning," I said.

"Tyler is coming to your class. I heard about you, and I am sick of that fool down the hall who couldn't care less about these kids."

"I would like that," I told her, "but my class is full, and I am not allowed to have more than thirty-two students."

"I already know that," she said. "There is a waiting list to get in here, but I can't wait no more. My boy can't read, and he in third grade already. Now they say you good. I need your help, and I ain't used to beggin' nobody for nothing, but I'm pleadin' and beggin'. Let him in."

Yolanda met with the school's principal and demanded that Tyler be placed in my class. He was admitted to my room the very next day.

Yolanda was a mother of three, and she had recently begun to turn her life around. She committed to her children's education with the hopes that a better life would follow. Because of this, Yolanda was incredibly grateful to me for trying to help her son. She promised me that she would ensure Tyler would submit all of his assignments.

I would learn over the next few months that Tyler was behind his grade level in every subject and was embarrassed by his inability to read. He would become outraged if anyone pointed it out. Other children used taunting and shaming words like *dummy* and *stupid* to put him down, which usually resulted in a playground or classroom fight.

Tyler and I were working diligently to increase his reading level. Whereas other children had small homework assignments that were a follow-up or extension of what was learned that day, Tyler would have an additional literacy assignment, such as reading fluency cards or phonemic awareness tapes. This additional assignment was more beneficial than I had expected, and Tyler continued to progress.

During Tyler's second month in my class, completed homework from him began to taper off. When he did turn in his work, I noticed some of it was coming in with shoddy presentation as well. How could this be? I remembered his mother's 110 percent commitment to her son's education and decided I needed to speak with Yolanda.

During our meeting, Yolanda mentioned that she had just taken on a night job to stay on top of her bills. She had three children to support—Tyler and his younger brother and sister. Because she couldn't keep as close of an eye on her children, she could no longer ensure they were doing their homework, although she had made them promise they would. Tyler's interest in homework was declining because of this change in his home life.

After inquiring about the children's evening routine, I quickly learned that there wasn't one. Basically Yolanda left dinner for them, and the children were supposed to complete their chores and home-work before going to bed. Yolanda arrived home around 9 p.m.

Yolanda and I both wanted Tyler to be successful, so I explained to her that what he likely needed was more structure at home. Although Tyler's literacy was improving, the pace would rapidly increase if he consistently completed his homework. Yolanda's initial response was much like any other parent in this community: "I'm gone whoop his you-know-what."

After agreeing that there were better alternatives to get buy-in from Tyler, she invited me to her home to observe and suggest methods of structure.

As I drove up, Yolanda greeted me on the porch and said, "I hope you are hungry." Inside her home, the smell of pork chops, mashed potatoes, and greens tickled my nose, and we all sat down to eat. Eating this delicious meal did not dissuade me from my focus. How was it that Tyler was in third grade and could not read, yet his mother was a passionate advocate at the school?

The school system had obviously failed this family, but this home visit revealed other issues that were keeping Tyler from getting on track. The interactions at dinner were like most homes where family dinners at the table no longer occur. Yolanda appeared uncomfortable with the raucous behavior of her three children, who were unfamiliar with the collaborative style of family dinners. Although it made Yolanda embarrassed since she had company, I realized this entire situation was unusual for the family due to Yolanda's work schedule and the children typically fending for themselves in the evening.

However, the lack of routine at dinnertime was not the focus of my interaction. It soon became obvious to me that the children had become used to giving excuses for uncompleted household chores and consequently had developed a lack of accountability. Over dinner I observed a conversation that demonstrated this exactly.

"Mama, Tyler didn't do his chores today. And he ran through the house and knocked over your vase and tried to cover it up by taping it back together," said Tyler's younger sister.

"Why you snitching?" asked Tyler.

"Yeah, snitch, snitch, you're a snitcher," chimed in Tyler's younger brother.

Tyler continued, "Mama, didn't you tell her to stop snitching so much? You know what happens to snitches in this neighborhood, girl."

Yolanda intervened by reprimanding Tyler's sister for snitching, and the boys smirked with delight. Did Yolanda even notice that she just got played by her two sons? The master manipulators were able to change and alter the conversation so that the focus was not on Tyler's failure to complete his chores or how he broke household furniture. Instead the conversation ended with punishment for "snitching." Was Yolanda even aware? I decided this scenario would serve as a lesson when speaking with Yolanda after dinner.

When it came time to share my thoughts with Yolanda that evening, she was eager to hear about better ways to provide structure for her children. She became slightly defensive and awestruck when I began to speak about what I had observed about her instead. I started this way:

"Ms. Anderson, it is obvious that you love your children. As a matter of fact, I wish all parents loved their children the way you do. It is apparent in the way you hug them and advocate for them in school. It is also apparent that you believe it is the school's job to educate your children. I agree with you, and I am here to challenge you. It is the school's responsibility to do just that! But we can only be successful with your help."

This is the moment Yolanda began to become defensive. "Okay, yeah, yeah, yeah, but what are you saying? Break it down and cut to the chase, because I know you are not about to say that I am the problem as to why my children are not learning."

Knowing that she would only accept a frank conversation at this point, I held back no punches.

"Ms. Anderson, you got to keep the main thing the main thing. Earlier tonight at dinner, I watched you allow your sons to get away with breaking household rules, and no one held them accountable. They believe they tricked you and got away with it. To you this may have nothing to do with why Tyler is not reading and is in third grade, but it does. He is not accountable for his learning."

"Wait, say that again?"

"Tyler is not accountable for his own learning?"

"Okay, I think I get that."

"Yes, just as he is not accountable for breaking that vase and not doing his chores. It's the same thing."

As Yolanda began to nod her head in agreement and understanding, I realized a breakthrough had just occurred. It was in this moment that I explained to Yolanda that one can have the best intentions in the world and still fail. Parents are not entirely to blame. Both children and parents must be held accountable for their actions. When a child misbehaves, consequences that don't involve whoopings are much more effective.

Yolanda understood. She and I got busy identifying how we could improve the children's home environment. Once we had a game plan, we worked to include activities she could use to both monitor and improve the structure of her home that allowed her children to stay engaged with her in the process. In each room, charts and graphic organizers identified chores, rewards earned, and time identification. Additionally a homework area was designated for each child. That child's schoolwork was posted in their area to make it special. Initially Tyler and his two siblings rebelled. But like an episode of *Supernanny*, follow-up was needed, and strong accountability was the prescription. When one child succeeded and got all their chores and homework done, a reward was given.

This certainly put the other two children on notice, as bragging was often involved. It only helped if the reward was something the children really wanted. An ice-cream-truck favorite, an extra hour of sleep on weekends, or a new clothing item served as great enticement for all to eventually get on board. Yolanda thought it was strange to bribe children into what they should be doing automatically, but once she began the system of rewarding one child, the others could not resist the temptation to earn a reward as well.

Understanding the importance of parental involvement at home is at the top of any teacher's wish list. Defining a home environment that facilitates a child's school success is a shortcut to a successful future, whether it be college or a career pathway. Parents who establish an academic home environment understand this.

Have high expectations of your students' parents. Although most school districts and school organizations frown on school mandates for parents, it does not mean you can't have expectations. Parent agreement contracts may sound formal, but they don't have to be. Most parents will welcome the opportunity to collaborate and be more involved with the success of their child in your school setting.

For children who are too young to attend school, parents and child care centers can work together to help develop children's social-emotional skills at home and at preschool. Parents should talk to their preschool about how children's social-emotional needs are being integrated into their daily routines and how they can get involved to help children learn important emotional lessons and navigate their environment more effectively.

Teachers everywhere recognize the importance of a solid connection between home and school and strive to build positive and respectful parent partnerships. All teachers understand the value of parents and the need for parent involvement and support, but not all parents can spend time in our classrooms, so establish some activities for parents to use at home that engage in the learning process.

The success of this school-home connection with Yolanda had a great ending. Because of our time spent together, which included my being invited to many family events throughout the years, I have become family, and Yolanda has become family to me. I am godfather to all three of her children, and she is godmother to my fourth-oldest son, Emmanuel. She has become the best example of a parent's efforts to advocate for their child. Yolanda, I salute you!

Embracing Family Culture

Every parent wants to know what their child is learning and how they are doing in school. One fun and informative way to keep parents connected to your classroom is through Friday letters. Every Friday have students write a letter or illustrate a drawing to take home to tell their parents and families all about their week at school. Ask the parents to respond by writing a letter or creating a drawing back to their child on the reverse side of the page. Students return the letters to school, where teachers file and save them. At the end of the year, bind all of their letters into keepsake books for students to take home.

Go outside, lie on your back, and look at the clouds with the children. Talk to them about the shapes they see. You will soon learn that a simple question like "What does it look like?" will turn into a lengthy conversation to build language and learn concepts.

Play a song you know. Then begin to tell the children a story that happened in your life. You don't have to tell the story exactly as you remember it—embellish a little, replacing the main character with your child or introducing a new character that will fascinate your child, like a dinosaur. Stop often and ask one of the children if they would like to add to the story.

The following activity is great for family dynamics. Parents and educators are also encouraged to use this activity at home and at school-based sites. Place four letter-size posters of four different animals on the wall. I suggest including a turtle, hawk, rabbit, and lion. Next ask the children to identify how they personally communicate. Give examples, such as "I am soft-spoken," "I am opinionated," "I will usually only talk to my friends," or "I love being silly." Ask the children to walk over to the sign that best represents which animal is most like them. They must only choose one. After choosing have the children explain their answers to the animal group they belong to, or partner share if the numbers are large. Each animal group will effectively be sharing the characteristics of its animal's communication style. Then each animal group or participant (based on size) will establish which other animal group they have the most difficult time communicating with based on their style. Here are a few examples:

- Turtles may be annoyed that lions are more aggressive or outspoken, and they value taking their time to speak.
- Lions may be annoyed that hawks simply hover and wait to speak when it is safe, yet they take risks and speak what comes to mind.
- Hawks may be annoyed that rabbits don't take matters seriously because they process information and analyze thoughts.
- Rabbits may be annoyed by turtles because of their pensive-like patience, yet they are quite free-spirited.

As they share these comparisons, remember that these communication styles are represented by the population, which will make the exercise more meaningful.

Find a traditional recipe from your culture and attempt to make the recipe as a family. Parents and children should partake in the traditional dish while discussing the heritage and ancestral background of the dish. For example, my mom's awesome lemon squares that we baked at Christmas were always a big highlight at my house. I look forward to holidays because of this special treat and the family bond it inspires. It also enlightened my understanding of how things get passed down from one generation to the next. Although I have never been to Scotland, my mom inherited her baking skills from her mother, and the recipe is derived from her Scottish heritage.

Reflections

☼ Whom in your life do you admire as a parent? Why?

☼ If you were to write a supportive statement to a parent of your choosing, what would you say?

☼ Recall a time when you were in the presence of a tender moment between a parent and a child. What happened?

☼ What can you say in the moment to a parent in the middle of a stressful situation with a child?

☼ What are the ways in your life that you have supported parenting?

☼ What can children teach parents?

☼ What can children teach teachers?

☼ What are the effects of family culture in your classroom?

☼ How do you develop relationships with families?

☼ What does it mean to be culturally responsive?

8 Questioning Behavior: The Moneymaker

WHAT PUSHES YOUR BUTTONS as an adult? Is it the child who ignores you or talks back? What about the child who tattletales or never stops talking? We each probably have one behavior that annoys us. I'll confess mine if you confess yours. The behavior I find most challenging in children is whining. It drives me nuts. I must also admit that in order to ensure a harmonious relationship with the child who possesses such behavior, I must consciously separate the behavior from the child. Why does it bother me so? My self-examination has led me to believe that the traits that bother us most as adults probably stem from things that occurred during our own childhood. It could be that you used to demonstrate this behavior, or perhaps you had some interaction with another child who did. This is certainly true of whining for me. Why? You guessed it. I was a whiner.

When I was a child, my brothers, who were older than me by two and three years, respectively, would go off to the store and leave me behind. My reaction was to whine as loudly as I could. As a young, spoiled child, I quickly learned that whining was the best tactic for receiving attention. It got me recognized early and often. My brothers, who were annoyed by the behavior, had no clue how to turn off my whining once I started. However, my mother was a professional at ignoring the behavior. I'm not sure if I grew out of it or if I decided that it no longer served its purpose, but eventually the attention I was seeking no longer came to me because of the whining.

I suggest to parents, teachers, and those who interact with children to identify the behavior or behaviors that work on your nerves. Remember to identify their roots because they may be stemming from your own childhood. If you demonstrated this behavior as well, consider what you sought to gain from it. Then seek to empathize with the child: why might this behavior be soothing for them?

I believe we are facing a national epidemic of children who are too spirited and exuberant for most people. Oftentimes adults are unprepared or unwilling to dig deeper when a child exhibits challenging behavior. Children have feisty, flexible, and fearless behaviors that must be harnessed and guided in positive directions. Otherwise, the results can be explosive and can also lead to wasted opportunities for genius. A perfect example is my daughter Faith.

Faith came into my life at two years of age. After her adoption, it was obvious what an amazing, resilient, and special child she would be. Unfortunately Faith was born with neonatal abstinence, which meant she was born with illegal drugs in her system. As a result, she suffered night terrors, a traumatic nightmare shaking state that affects young children born with drugs in their system. Although most would consider this a huge deficit for a child, Faith's resilience was noticed early on.

I like to think that there are three types of people in this world: some tap on the window to be let in, some knock on the door, and some kick down anything that gets in their way. Undoubtedly the third option is how Faith came into this world. Although she suffered from the effects of withdrawal, she amazed everyone in the family. Curious and precocious, Faith's rocky start did not hold her back. She was a quick learner and excelled at a faster pace than any of my other four children. She was the poster child for the mantra "the journey to college graduation begins in preschool," for Faith was cultivating a college-going mindset from a very young age.

Yes, Faith was quite a child. At just two years old, she was reciting poems and channeling Beyoncé and President Obama—what powerful choices. When Faith was three years old, she politely told her eight-year-old brother in the middle of dinner that he would have to find another place to live if he could not be more loving to her. She was respected by her friends for her leadership and earned the nickname President Faith. My family called her Baby Oprah, for she was and still is assured, resilient, and divine. Her vision and insight were way beyond her years, and in the family circle, we joked, "That girl been here befo'!" Her psychoanalysis of situations and events typically had listeners in awe. She was amazing and bold, but occasionally her brilliance and forethought created trouble.

While she was adored by peers and family members, school staff found Faith to be a challenge because of her sneakiness. Some would consider her a child with challenging behaviors (a challenging behavior is any repeated pattern of behavior that interferes with learning or engagement in social interactions). Challenging behaviors during the preschool years can sometimes predict later, more serious problem behaviors including delinquency, aggression, and antisocial behavior. Thus the challenge for educators and parents is to address social-emotional behaviors early on so that children are developing appropriately for their age group.

Every child has different behavioral norms. As an educator, I knew that a child's temperament determined the adult's perception of that child. I hoped Faith's behaviors would not come across as disruptive or troublemaking. I was worried about Faith's behavior at school and wanted to better prepare for any upcoming challenges. Although I was fascinated by her unpredictable behavior, which often resulted in uncontrollable laughter, it could certainly push the wrong buttons in a classroom setting. Would any repeated pattern of behavior interfere with learning or engagement in prosocial interactions with peers or adults? In an effort to learn more about challenging behavior, I offered to instruct a continuing course on that very subject at the university where I teach.

The benefits of teaching this course were twofold: I educated other professionals, and I learned and incorporated new strategies and methods for my daughter. My greatest takeaway from teaching this course was my realization that there is a difference between misbehavior and mistaken behavior. I also learned that active children are most comfortable being active. Armed with this knowledge, I felt confident that I was helping set Faith up for success.

Then, when Faith was six years old, she came face to face with her worst nightmare to date. It was Ms. Perkins, the teacher all children at Wilmington Road Elementary School hated the most. Looking much older than her actual age of sixty-two, Ms. Perkins wasn't known for smiling. In fact some said she had never been seen smiling . . . ever! She was stern and old school and believed in tough discipline and punishment when children misbehaved. Yes, stern and tough Ms. Perkins was—that is, until she met Faith. A life lesson was about to be learned by both.

Faith learned of her enrollment in Ms. Perkins's first-grade class over the summer, and she spent countless hours during June, July, and August attempting to bribe me into having her transferred out of Ms. Perkins's class.

"I'll do dishes every day," she would say, or, "What about I promise to get all As?"

"I can polish your shoes" was another one.

Two weeks before the end of summer, she tried pleading with anything that she thought would get her out of becoming a student in Ms. Perkins's classroom. I explained to her that success is in the future of anyone who can adapt to our nation's diverse group of people. I also told Faith that we are all different and unique, from our personality to our culture, and she would most likely encounter various types of people in college, the workplace, and elsewhere. She would need to learn how to not be negatively affected by them.

After shrugging her shoulders and watering her eyes, she returned to her room, but not before pronouncing, "I hope she ready for me then."

"First grade," I remember reflecting. OMG!

The beginning of the school year came and went. Faith and Ms. Perkins must have gotten along okay because there were no big disasters. Then came the incident that I affectionately call the Ice Cream Truck Story. I was at work when I received a phone call from Ms. Perkins. She asked if I could come to the school immediately. She told me there was an issue with Faith but that it was not proper to discuss the situation over the phone. Every parent dreads a phone call like this one. I took a deep breath, gathered my things, and headed to the school. I was nervous the entire way. I didn't know what the issue was, but I assumed it was major if I was being asked to come to the school. The only thing I could think of was that perhaps Faith had been sent to the principal's office. I had been sent there as a child myself, and I remembered that dreadful feeling as if it were yesterday.

The good news was that when I got to the school, Faith was not in the principal's office. I headed to Ms. Perkins's room. I had met Ms. Perkins twice before, once on the first day of school and again during the classroom open house, but I had heard countless stories of her meanness from Faith. I knocked on Ms. Perkins's room door, and she welcomed me in.

As I walked into the room, my immediate focus was to find Faith. This was difficult because all the lights were out. Glancing around the room, I noticed she was sitting at her desk. Her head was down, but her eyes were raised and protruded over her elbows. She looked stunned. I turned around and looked at Ms. Perkins. Faith was right—she was quite intimidating. Ms. Perkins was elderly and wrinkled, and she had a permanent frown that I thought might be tattooed. For a moment, my silliness helped me relax.

The moment didn't last. Ms. Perkins said, "Well, do you want to know what she did?"

"Yes, I do."

"Please follow me."

We exited the classroom and went through an adjacent door to an empty classroom. Just as I began to wonder why we left the other room, Ms. Perkins spoke.

"Never in all my years have I met a child like yours, Mr. Haggood. Yesterday I learned after school that Faith was stealing other children's monies."

I was shocked. Faith could be smart and slick but stealing? It was very out of character for her.

As Ms. Perkins explained, it became clear that what Faith had done could definitely be called theft. In fact embezzlement might be more accurate.

First Faith had designed a flyer that promoted an ice cream truck item, a special ring lollipop that changed colors once licked. She showed her friends the poster and told them all to bring fifty cents to school. She told them that her uncle was the ice cream truck driver and she could get a discount from him. The problem was that this item really cost twenty-five cents, so Little Miss Profit was about to clean up. I was flabbergasted. Who does this in first grade? I thought.

Ms. Perkins continued, "I was talking with Faith and lecturing her about fooling people and that although she is smart, she did a bad thing. Well, as I am lecturing her, I tell her that I am going to have to call her dad. Mr. Haggood, as I am telling her this . . ."

Ms. Perkins paused, and I noticed that she was beginning to laugh. Wait . . . was that . . . no . . . yes, it was a smile!

"After I told her that I will have to call you, Mr. Haggood, Faith got up out of her chair and closed the door and said, 'Ms. Perkins, you don't need to call him. We can handle this right here, you and me. He's real busy, and I know if we put our minds together, we can solve this.'"

By this point, Ms. Perkins was laughing with her hand over her mouth so Faith would not hear her from in the other room.

"I'm sorry, Mr. Haggood, that girl is something else, and I know I shouldn't laugh, but I have never had a child who thoroughly amuses me. She is hilarious." She laughed again. "So yes, she did fool the children, and we will go next door and pretend to be outraged by her behavior, but honestly it is quite genius."

I was shocked. First that Faith could orchestrate such a thing and second that Ms. Perkins was not only smiling but laughing as well! The two of us agreed upon consequences for Faith and entered the classroom to explain them to her. Afterward I was asked to stay in the room for a few minutes.

We had just spent several minutes focusing on Faith, but now Ms. Perkins addressed me. "We must take the time to try to understand children's feelings and what children are trying to communicate through their behavior. I know you are upset, but if we take a step back and look at this thing from a different view, it is quite genius and funny. She used persuasion, problem-solving skills, and was able to calculate a profit. Quite impressive." Was this Ms. Perkins? I couldn't believe it.

This interaction forever changed the way I think about teachers learning from their students. Ms. Perkins's glass half-full approach and perception of the situation allowed me to see and interact with Faith differently. Although Faith surprised me on many occasions with her antics, it was Ms. Perkins who recognized her energy as "gifted" first.

Without Ms. Perkins's perspective, I may have neglected to appreciate some of Faith's skills. So how do we recognize, redirect, and more importantly celebrate challenging behavior in students? It is important to find the positives in a child's challenging behavior and to encourage those positives. This is just one of the things Faith has taught me over the years.

Many years later, when Faith competed in her first debate at the University of Southern California, her ability to influence and succeed was evident. As I sat there watching her debate that memorable morning, I beamed with pride. Faith had asserted her arguments against juniors and seniors and won. I couldn't help but think about where her power of persuasion began—in Ms. Perkins's first-grade classroom.

Encourage Positive Behavior

Decorate a tissue box with arts and crafts materials so that it becomes a treasure box. Fill the box with items the children can benefit from, such as pencils, crayons, stickers, markers, or other classroom items. Use this box to encourage positive behavior in children. When a child does something positive, let them select a reward from the treasure box.

Have students complete sentence prompts that encourage the behavior you want them to recognize and exhibit: "I like it when I _____." "I appreciate _____ about myself." "Whenever I _____ I get positive praise."

Have an end-of-day meeting to reflect on how children behaved that day and how they can improve their behavior in the future. Notice and support the ownership of traits and behaviors. The intention of this exercise is to focus on improving a child's behavior, not judging it.

Children who have little experience with school tend to show up very excited, which can be draining. In order to keep them focused and in control of their own behavior, I initiated "sticker time." If by the end of the day a student did not need a reminder to focus and was a good listener, they received a small sticker. To keep this incentive fun, it's important to change it up. After using "sticker time" daily for several months, I changed the activity so that my students could only earn a sticker on Friday afternoons if they had behaved all week.

Create phrases or signals that students and teacher can use to reference positive behavior. For example, "kiss your brain" may be a wonderful way to praise a smart comment. It is also a good idea to have phrases that signal to children when it is time to focus. "Hocus, pocus, focus" may be a call to get attention in the classroom. The teacher calling "one, two" and the class responding "eyes on you" is a great way to have students initiate positive focus when the teacher needs cooperation.

Reflections

☼ What might a child's tantrum be telling you in the moment?

☼ When children display challenging behavior, what emotions come up for you?

☼ Is there something about your culture or family background that makes you more or less tolerant of certain kinds of behaviors?

☼ Is your temperament similar to or very different from the child you're concerned about?

☼ Why do you think it is hard for children with aggressive behavior to succeed in school?

☼ What other problems can aggressive behavior create for children?

☼ How does the quality of care, parental and non-parental, influence brain development?

☼ What role does caregiving play in managing stress?

☼ In what ways does your attitude affect your ability to use an appropriate intervention?

☼ What activities do you use to inspire positive behavior from children?

9 Learning Relationships: The Language of Laughter

CREATING A SAFE AND ENRICHING CLASSROOM environment starts with you. Yes, aesthetic furniture, appealing decorations, and colorful bulletin boards add to the positive environment. However, the most important aspect in cultivating a positive climate begins with you.

It's up to you to make your students feel welcomed and celebrated. Having a positive relationship with each student makes you a better teacher. When teachers strive to engage students in a discussion or an activity, their interactions with those students speak volumes about the extent to which they value the relationship.

A teacher's goal is to be effective in the classroom and help students learn. Educators want their students to be inspired, eager, and engaged. Humor has the power to inspire and fuel that engagement. When teachers share a laugh or a smile with students, they help students feel more comfortable and open to learning. It can help children stay focused on the lesson, and sometimes it even helps them stay motivated or remember ideas. Using humor brings enthusiasm, positive feelings, and optimism to the classroom.

I have shared this belief with many people over the years, including the college students I teach at National University on Tuesday nights. As an instructional professor, my major goal is always the same: I want my students to remember the saying "The best teachers are those who have the best relationships with their students." This does not take an outing to the coffee shop or a visit to their Little League game, but it does take making a concentrated effort to treat them well, encourage them, and figure out how they learn. I remind my college students that the student who challenges you the most is stretching your skills as an educator. Some of my students, deep in the trenches and geared up for rigorous teaching battles, consider this nonsense. Some, for instance, believe in a more conventional style of teaching with all of its traditional approaches. This style may be all they know if it's what they experienced as students themselves. No matter what, I continue to encourage future educators to use laughter to build relationships with their students.

I do this because using laughter to enhance relationships with students *works*. Humor can be an effective way to engage students and activate learning. Teachers can use humor to bring early childhood subject matter to life. Students respond to a teacher's playful games, jokes, or strange character voices and appreciate the effort they put into making a lesson fun. When a teacher decides to share their sense of humor, whether by standing up on a desk, playing tag with students at recess, or rapping a song full out with hand gestures, it humanizes the teacher and makes them more relatable to the students. Creating a comfortable and positive learning environment can increase a child's optimism about their own learning. Too often parents and teachers create a pressure-filled environment where children don't feel safe, and this can negatively affect learning.

Many years ago, I learned firsthand just how much humor can positively affect a child's life. James Bernard was a first-grade student newly arrived from France. He was enrolled in our school by his father, a serious man who was not afraid to voice his educational expectations. From the start, Mr. Bernard made it clear that James was to listen, obey, and perform tasks. He insisted that James pay attention without any behavioral incident. Mr. Bernard had robotic demands and requirements of James, and he did not see the value of learning through play. Eventually he conceded that some play would be necessary for James's development, but not until after I informed him that our staff would need to build language through play since English was James's second language.

Each day James would exit his dad's car, enter the school site, and not say a word for several hours. Rigid and tense, James would only observe other students; he would never interact with them. Any child who attempted to play with James quickly learned, either through facial scowls or complete silence, that they were not welcome in his world. James was good at getting the message across that he wanted to be left alone.

The staff and I wrote a thorough plan of action for James's education. We attempted to include Mr. Bernard, but he was uninterested and would not show up to meetings. Ultimately we settled on three strategies we thought would make a difference: staging the lesson, using even more manipulatives than normal, and using an extra teaching assistant to model expected learning. Boy were we wrong. James was unresponsive to any of the techniques we used. After three weeks of implementing our strategies, we realized we were not making an impact on James. We were disappointed because we had thought our strategies would work; they had worked for other students in the past. We hadn't even managed to get James to open up slightly. It was time to adjust our methods.

Then, as if we were being rewarded for our efforts, a change in James occurred—and it had nothing to do with our strategies. The change arrived on Beautification Day, a special event where staff and students work together to enrich our campus environment. Planting flowers, picking up litter, and painting were some of the activities planned. To add to the event and to highlight the significance of a clean, safe, and pleasant environment, we invited a few clowns to our event.

The transformation happened once James sighted the clowns. We heard laughter for the first time, and he even attempted to speak. His face lit up and his expressions were meaningful. At first we thought it was the clowns' physical appearance that attracted James's attention. We would soon learn that it was not the clown's makeup or clothing; it was our special education assistant Ms. Lewis who realized it was the behavior of the clown that was attracting James. Our staff got busy. We decided to explore reaching James through social-emotional expressions. We yearned for the laugh that James shared so freely with the clowns.

From that day forward, we decided to laugh, smile, and play with intention. Multiple times a day, we purposely included an opportunity for laughter. Initially, just like all children, James responded with a gaze as if he had figured us out. His expression showed he was sizing us up to see if we were just acting or pretending. His observance was focused, just like the kind of focus great teachers have when observing students. Even when I, the principal, would come in the classroom and smile and laugh with the children, he remained razor sharp in his observance. Were we acting? Were we pretending? Could we keep up this level of performance? The staff was determined to win this battle.

It did not take long. When they noticed a slight laugh from James, the staff praised and affectionately responded to James. He smiled broadly. The breakthrough had happened. The only sad thing was that I missed it. Over the next few days and months, it would be the talk of the teachers' lounge.

James's progress had been a school-wide mission. He taught us something about ourselves as educators that was more valuable than any curriculum plan or college course. Because of James, the staff approached joy with intention, not just with James but with each child. It became our focus to allow them to see our humanity. We collectively decided that once we got out of our individual cars in the school parking lot and entered the school gates, we were on sacred ground. This sometimes meant we had to put on a performance. Even when staff members showed up to work with issues in their personal lives, we recognized that our children needed to see us smile, laugh, and dance. James helped us realize that when children see our adult faces and larger bodies, they may not see our normalness.

We began talking and sharing more about our own families, vacations, and celebrations, which resonated with our children. Laughter filled our classrooms and hallways. The ripple effect of happiness even reached Mr. Bernard. On one occasion when the staff welcomed James to school with the warmest of embraces, they noticed a slight slant of Mr. Bernard's mouth that could be mistaken for a smile.

My students have taught me some valuable lessons over the years. Laughter in the classroom has become one of the most important tools in my educational profession. Whether I am about to speak in front of three hundred people at a professional conference or I am working with students in a classroom, I use laughter to engage my audience. I think laughter is an invaluable part of every early childhood program.

Who knows how much of an impact this positive learning environment had on James's education? Who knows how much it affected his father? What I do know is that it benefited James's ability to interact with others. This experience helped James become more comfortable with everyone around him. His peers were receptive to James's new persona and were much more open to playing and speaking with him. Whereas before I would never see James playing freely or starting a conversation with a peer, it was now happening readily.

I wonder how many adults have seen their parents laugh or cry or heard them say they love them. While this behavior may be very normal for some, the number of people affected by not seeing their parents display human emotion may surprise you. I am not sure if Mr. Bernard ever realized how much his emotional stoicism affected James. However, I am certain that if adults were less guarded with their children, it would have a huge impact on their lives and in the process allow the child to be more successful at home and at school.

All teachers and parents can learn something from James's story. Children learn from us, but acknowledging that children do in fact teach us as well is key. Because of James's teaching, teachers began to joke, sing, dance, and even shout. So stand up on that desk and tap dance, or sing that homework assignment. Try role-playing the characters in a funny story. Finding humor in everyday situations will create laughter and build positive relationships. Laugh at home and at school. The benefits are yours.

Humor in the Classroom

Ask the children in your classroom to role-play the characters in a funny story, or have them make up their own story. For example, some of the children could be patrons at a restaurant and other children could be the servers, or they could role-play going to the dentist, the movies, or the zoo. The possibilities are endless.

Stand in a circle and have the children think of a word they think is funny. It could be a small or a large word depending on the ages of the students. Ask them to think of a silly gesture to accompany their word. Then go around the circle and have the children share.

Most students associate laughter and fun with outdoor play. Switch it up and create indoor play activities that boost laughter and relieve your classroom stress, especially before a big test or other tense situation. For example, have children make up dances or share dance moves with the rest of the class.

Facilitate a game of "Two Truths and a Lie" with the children in your care. Write down two factual funny stories or statements about you. Make up the third statement or story. Then read all three statements aloud and ask listeners to guess which one is not true.

Show children pictures of animals or sea creatures. Have them identify something that comes to mind when they look at the picture. For example, an octopus could remind them of an alien, a picture of jellyfish could remind them of slime, or a picture of a wrinkled puppy could look like their bath towel when it's rolled up.

Reflections

☼ What benefits do children gain when adults display laughter?

☼ How can a busy teacher find time for humor in the classroom?

☼ Do you allow space for moments of laughter in your classroom? At home?

☼ What kind of atmosphere does a lighthearted workplace create?

☼ What would happen if you laughed more in the workplace?

☼ Who in your life can you turn to when you need a laugh?

☼ Have you ever laughed in a moment of stress? What did you gain?

☼ How do you respond to laughter?

☼ What do you feel when you are having fun?

☼ What do you feel when you see others having fun?

10 Great Expectations: My Hero

MOST TEACHERS ARE HEROES. Notice I said most, not all. Every profession has those employees who simply show up for a paycheck. Then there are those teachers who go above and beyond, who deeply care about their students and want them to be successful. In a world of educational heroes, I have one of my own. Her name is Ms. Lovery. She has all the traits of inspirational educational leaders: she is persistent and caring, and she has an unwavering commitment to a system that has far too much bureaucracy and not enough focus on children.

I met Ms. Lovery in my first year as a principal. African American, around forty, short, and full of vibrant energy, she tested me and stretched my learning far more than any other teacher I have encountered. She was a preschool special education teacher with vast knowledge and possessed a tool kit of fascinating strategies for special needs children. At the time, I saw her inaccurately as a complainer. Now I know that she was an advocate. Her advocacy grew over time, but as a first-year principal, it was hard to recognize at first.

As principal I had an open-door policy; teachers and students were encouraged to stop by my office any time with thoughts or concerns.

Ms. Lovery frequently came to my office, something I once saw as redundant but now see as purposeful, with the goal of rallying me to her cause. She would start off each visit to my office by sharing a triumphant fact, something like "Mr. Haggood, did you know Bill Gates's first business failed?"

"No, I didn't know that," was my customary response.

Then Ms. Lovery would begin advocating for her students. Sometimes she had specific requests, such as "We need a new feeding table for children who need more range in dropping food when they eat." After some children ate, their clothing reeked for the rest of the day due to all of the food they spilled on themselves.

Other times her requests were more broad. "Do we have enough in our budget to purchase a new adaptive physical therapist for the children?" I knew these types of requests came from a place of genuine care for her students. Typically the answer would be no based on the laughable budget we had for anything extra, but I was always impressed that she bothered to ask. Her intentions were purposeful and challenging.

Over time I realized that Ms. Lovery was not coming to my office to simply receive a yes or no; she was planting a seed. Her intention was for me to take my work more seriously. If I answered her requests with a no, then what would we do? The need was still there, and the need was for the children, our students. Every time I turned down Ms. Lovery's requests, the seed she planted grew until it became an issue I could no longer ignore.

Ms. Lovery sparked a dialogue that I began to have in my head as the principal and school's leader. What was I doing to challenge the whys of the school system? The real needs of students should result in yes, always. This made me reflect on an issue that began at my school long before I became principal: a feud over the placement of special education students in the preschool general education world. With time I managed to carefully massage this tense situation into a win-win for both programs (special and general education). However, I was still met with unhappiness from both sides. The general education staff asked questions like "Why are we letting severe special education students in with the regular children? Isn't this dangerous?" More than fifteen pilot preschool collaborative programs closed due to nonacceptance of particular communities and staff. Even though my leadership had helped the school turn some corners, I learned that there was always more work to be done. Because of this experience, I was empathetic to Ms. Lovery's plight.

Ms. Lovery was incredibly passionate about one of her students in particular, Gloria Uzo. Gloria had Down syndrome, and she was placed in our educational facility in my third month as principal. Most children like Gloria were placed in special needs classrooms instead of inclusion programs like ours, so how she ended up in our program was a mystery at first. Yet there she was. (Later the staff learned that Gloria's mother, an African single mom, was unaware of special needs programs within large school districts and simply enrolled Gloria in the program closest to her job.)

Gloria was three, and she quickly became our most challenging child to date. In the early days of her enrollment, she regularly threw objects, yelled, and swung to engage. Gloria's violent outbursts were typical of a child with severe needs who was placed in a strange environment, but the fears of my staff, who were not trained to care for children with severe needs, began to creep up. "We love Gloria," they would say, "but how can we manage when she can't even speak?"

Over the next few weeks, I observed as the possibility of Gloria leaving our program became a probable reality. The district started drafting papers that would leave Gloria's mom with no alternative but to enroll Gloria in a different program. Before these papers could be finalized, however, I learned that Ms. Uzo and Gloria weren't going anywhere without a fight.

During a meeting I had with Ms. Uzo, she informed me that she had no intention of leaving the school. She told me that my school was providing her daughter with what she needed the most—love! Ms. Uzo said she would wage war with the school district if she had to. I found myself in a tough position. On one hand, as the administrator of the school, was I doing a disservice to my staff members by allowing a child who was clearly not able to collaborate with others to stay at the school? Or was I doing a disservice to this parent and child who had found an academic home, a safe space created with love? I was conflicted, but I felt proud that a parent so desperately wanted their child to remain in my program.

The day after I spoke with Ms. Uzo, Ms. Lovery entered my office in the usual way.

"Did you know that Albert Einstein didn't speak until he was four years old?"

"No, I didn't know that," I replied.

Ms. Lovery soon got to her point. She had come to my office to talk about the future of Gloria's care. Ms. Lovery was one staff member who never wavered in her support of Gloria. Although I had not yet made a decision about Gloria's position in the program, Ms. Lovery began to thank me for letting Gloria stay. With tears in her eyes and a rasp in her throat, she thanked me on behalf of the hundreds of children who needed a place to *be*, as she put it.

It was in that moment that I remembered that Ms. Lovery herself had a special needs child. That child was now a teenager, and she had mentioned her child on a few occasions. Gloria's position in the program had special meaning for Ms. Lovery. As she left my office, she turned and said, "Did you know that Jim Carrey used to be homeless and Steven Spielberg was rejected from USC twice?"

It was at this time that the seeds Ms. Lovery had planted really began to blossom. I started hearing (not simply listening to) Ms. Lovery and her advocacy. It was she who smiled and talked with Gloria during the special elaborate feeding system that Gloria's disability demanded. She felt that purposeful social-emotional engagement was an undervalued interaction between adults and children in the preschool world.

This was the reminder I needed: a real-life example of the impact a positive preschool education could have on a child. Over the years, I have noticed an increase in the promotion of preschool and the huge difference it makes in a child's development and education. This focus on preschool importance has appeared in many forms. Billboards, articles, and television commercials have been overwhelmingly informative of the value of preschool for brain development and environmental influence in children ages zero to five years old. President Barack Obama listened quite well and funneled never-before-seen funding in this direction. In his State of the Union address in 2013, he correctly pointed out the benefits of preschool education investment: boosting graduation rates, reducing teen pregnancy, reducing crime, increasing the likelihood of reading and doing math at grade level, holding a job, and contributing to more stable homes. A preschool education could make all the difference, especially for a student like Gloria.

Thanks to Ms. Lovery's constant support, I, for the first time, began to see Gloria's future. I was waking up to my own ignorance; I had been thinking about Gloria's future all wrong. During classroom observations or interactions with students, I typically visualized future lawyers, actors, and scientists. I used to question if I could visualize Gloria working or holding a job. But I was overlooking the most important thing: Gloria was progressing. Her skills were developing, and she was responding to positive praise. Her rapid responses to simple requests were increasing. Since the beginning of the school year, simple tasks that we had initially viewed as yearly goals had to be discarded for new, more expansive goals. Feeding herself, listening to others, and sharing with friends were developmental measures that Gloria was now completing with ease.

The decision was made that Gloria would continue on in our program. It was not long before the staff began to ask what academic expectations we had for her. You already know who led the charge.

Ms. Lovery entered the office and stated, "Ben Franklin dropped out of school at age ten, and Stephen King's first novel was rejected thirty times. Did you know that?"

After I responded with the usual "No, I didn't know that," Ms. Lovery presented her purpose for coming to my office.

"Dr. Haggood, I believe we are not fulfilling our best intentions with Gloria. What are our academic expectations? She has fulfilled and surpassed our social-emotional expectations, but that is not enough. I believe that Gloria can do some of the same things that the other children in class are doing. And I don't mean just getting along. I want to see her be able to write, read, and solve problems in science and math just like the others. I know she can do it. I see it in her."

I began to reflect on our successes with Gloria's education. Assume nothing and learn everything was our philosophy. As much as we wanted to assume certain things about Gloria, we needed to put our assumptions on hold and allow her to show us what she could achieve.

With the second semester beginning, I agreed with Ms. Lovery's intentions to push Gloria's academic abilities. Together we created an individualized education plan for Gloria and decided to assess her skill development weekly in order to facilitate heightened awareness of benchmark progress. We were careful not to make sweeping generalizations or stereotypes. Decisions would be made based solely on observation. When we made observations about Gloria's behavior, we followed up that observation with a question: "You seem to work well in a group, but when you work independently, you become agitated. Can you help me understand why that is?" We realized this razor-sharp focus would be doing other children a service as well, and it quickly became a part of our everyday interactions with students. This approach forced us to make time to get to know each child. It was a humbling reminder that each child is different although they may seem comparable to others.

Within two months, Gloria was excelling just like Ms. Lovery hypothesized. She was responding on request, holding a pencil longer than usual, and attempting to scribble, and most of all, she was loving school. With the hope of not stereotyping all children with Down syndrome, I tell you that a surefire way to feel joy was to notice Gloria smiling. Her smile was not just radiant but the sun itself. All of us loved watching her grow.

The end of the school year was approaching, and Gloria was on track to hit and exceed her academic expectations. Best of all, with Ms. Lovery modeling best-practice strategies, the entire staff was on board with contributing to Gloria's progress. It was an awesome display of a true team working together to impact a life.

One day that spring, I noticed Ms. Lovery headed toward my office.

"Did you know that Oprah Winfrey gave birth at age fourteen and lost her child and that Charlize Theron witnessed her mother kill her father?"

"No, I didn't know that, Ms. Lovery."

At this moment, Ms. Lovery asserted her final request on behalf of the student she loved so much.

"I want Gloria to recite the flag salute at our culmination this year."

I responded, "Do you think she can? Oh, I would love that."

Ms. Lovery was shocked by my immediate support. I reminded her that it was she who taught me to remove any limitations I set for Gloria.

June was approaching. I was aware that Gloria was practicing with staff and family in preparation for her leading the flag salute. Could she do it? I always anticipated a wonderful culmination complete with celebrations of staff and students. However, no one could have prepared me for the epic moment I was about to witness.

The day of the culmination was similar to all others. Festive colors graced the auditorium, and parents and loved ones showed up with balloons and stuffed animals. Even though I reminded parents that this was a culmination and not a graduation, attempting to downplay the value of the event never worked. It was usually the first formal achievement event for their children, and although they were four-year-olds, it was always amazing how much energy was put into the event.

The auditorium was packed. Due to the rush of the morning and so many production moments, I was only able to check in with Ms. Lovery once. When she saw me, she said, "You can introduce a concept, but you can't force acceptance."

I interpreted this to mean we had done our part and the rest was up to Gloria. Predicting what would occur was impossible. Gloria was able to recite her lines in front of her classmates, but during the dress rehearsal, Gloria froze with the microphone in her hands. Gloria remembering the salute while standing in front of a packed room full of energized adults was perhaps asking for too much. Or was it?

The moment was upon us. The staff was all dressed up and standing with their students, watching anxiously. The auditorium was loud with anticipation. Under the bright lights, Ms. Lovery walked Gloria to stand next to me on stage. Gloria wore a beautiful white dress. When the audience saw her, they realized the big moment.

"Families, staff, and students of this school community, welcome to our annual prekindergarten culmination." The audience applauded. "Please welcome one of the students we are most proud of this year, Gloria Uzo." This time, the applause was thunderous.

Without a hitch, Gloria moved her mouth toward the mic.

"Hi, everybody," she said. The audience let out a collective sigh. "Please stand."

OMG, I thought. It is happening. She is doing it.

"Put your . . . your hand on heart."

The entire auditorium began the pledge.

"I pledge allegiance . . ."

It was then that I looked around the room to receive the full blessing of the moment. There was not a dry eye in the house. It was not just the staff who loved Gloria; the parents had come to care for her just as much while dropping off and picking up their own children. Staff and parents alike were hugging, crying, and attempting to make it through the pledge respectfully. In this moment, I felt deeply appreciative for the parents in the audience. After all they had never complained about Gloria's differences. Certainly, at the time of enrollment, it would not have been hard to imagine several of them raising questions about Gloria being in the program.

Halfway through the pledge of allegiance, I lost it as well.

Ms. Lovery walked over to me with a grin and whispered in my ear, "Dr. Haggood, did you know that Gloria Uzo is a student with Down syndrome?"

Over the course of that eventful school year, Ms. Lovery and Gloria Uzo taught the staff not to let our fears of the unknown derail us. We came together to change the life of one little girl. Because of Ms. Lovery's heartfelt commitment to reaching children and overcoming obstacles, I was witness to the miraculous power of a teacher's love. This story affirms that the way to a child's brain is to unlock their heart!

No child can learn from you if they feel you are not interested in them. Each moment either strengthens or diminishes a relationship. Make time to ask the children in your care about their hobbies, likes, and dislikes. Eat lunch with a student, imitate a trendy dance, and ask questions that show you're truly interested in them. Most important, lead with a positive emotion whenever you interact with a child. Whether their behavior is erratic or appropriate, your disposition matters. You must be the example you want to see in them.

No matter how great you believe your lesson plan or presentation is, your students will not perform if they do not respect and trust you. That respect and trust is built over time and is rooted in children feeling supported, safe, and honored in your care.

Finally, remember to set expectations that make it possible for a child to enhance their abilities. It only takes one person to believe what others may not see.

High Expectations

Make it a goal to put on a monthly play in your classroom. Based on that month's student performance, children are given tickets to be either an audience member or a character in the play. Roles are assigned based on teacher identification of student need. For example, a teacher may give a shy-but-on-task student a ticket to star in the play in the hopes that it will help them come out of their shell.

Preschool students are developmentally focused on self. Having them grow in the social-emotional area is important. Ask preschool students to do something nice for a friend in the class. For example, they could make their friend an art project. Physical gifts are not necessary; verbal gifts can be given as well.

In the classroom, establish a performance chart right next to a growth chart so that students make the correlation that both are growing all the time. Measure children using the growth chart and performance chart throughout the year.

Build an obstacle course at school or at home, which allows for each child's physical abilities to expand and develop. Then watch children build and exceed their expectations. You can do this by setting a variable time limit during an activity, which will help children see growth over time and promote healthy competition, or by adding an extra tire to the tire course for children to step in and out of.

Research stories about notable real-life people who overcame tremendous obstacles. You could also research historical events where obstacles were overcome. Good examples include Dr. King and the civil rights movement, as well as Derek Redmond's touching Olympic moment with his father. Share the stories you have chosen with the children. After discussing each story, have children share something they have overcome.

Reflections

☼ How do you strengthen relationships with your students or children?

☼ Who is your unsung hero? How can you honor them?

☼ Has anyone in your life served as your Ms. Lovery, the person who reaffirms your calling and allows you to keep your perspective? What about this person has helped you the most?

☼ What qualities do people who help others have?

☼ Describe a time you felt discriminated against. Was it in a school setting?

☼ What do you say to yourself when you feel you haven't been as open as you intended to be?

☼ Describe how it feels when you help a child learn and grow past others' expectations.

☼ How does it feel when you see children exceed their expectations?

☼ What happens to witnesses when they experience a moment like Gloria's speech in the auditorium?

11 Recognizing Trauma: The Reactor

ASK ANY ADMINISTRATOR OR TEACHER in the country what our top priority is for students and families, and their response will most likely be providing a safe environment. A serious crisis at any early childhood program cannot just obstruct the instructional program, but it can also reveal a serious fracture in the overall operational functions of a school. School-site personnel spend countless hours training and preparing for things they hope will never happen. Like any school district, safety policies and resources exist for the Los Angeles Unified School District. Although these resources are informative and cover a wide range of subjects, most schools spend time on policies that cover common safety precaution occurrences and leave it at that. Fire drills, earthquake preparedness, and lockdown procedures are average, readily available trainings provided for adults who care for children.

In most early childhood programs, there are many operational systems that include detailed walkthroughs of what to do when there is a crisis situation and the safety of a child is at risk. Various scenarios are considered in the walkthrough material, since many things could be considered a crisis situation. Each staff member is assigned individual duties and responsibilities during a crisis situation, and these are practiced monthly at location sites. Depending on the subject of the training, they may occur annually. Our school's crisis plan would only be put into action if something of major importance disrupted an otherwise average day. Although it may seem unlikely, crisis situations are happening at an alarming rate. Take, for example, the recent gun violence on many campuses in our nation. It is important that educators are prepared for all possibilities.

Although there is extensive preparation for a potential crisis, I was always quite aware that a typical early childhood crisis situation was a strange weather occurrence. I had never had any reason to use the crisis unit and our site crisis team plan, except for the emotional incident when one of my most beloved staff members had a heart attack on our site one Monday morning. Then, in my fourth year as principal, a serious crisis situation occurred.

This major disruption involved a single mother, Ms. Stram, and her three sons, two of whom were enrolled in our preschool program. The oldest of the three boys had already moved on to the kindergarten program at the adjoining elementary campus. I was fond of this family because it reminded me of my family unit. I am the youngest of three boys, and my mom, like Ms. Stram, was fiercely dedicated to her "babies," what she called us whenever she referred to us as a group. I would watch the Stram family pass my office with a morning greeting of "Hello, Dr. Haggood," and smile in remembrance of my youth and fond memories with my mom and brothers. I was most interested in the youngest Stram boy, since I, too, was the youngest. Mikey had recently enrolled in our preschool program and had just turned three. He was a quiet child and developmentally on track except for a few sudden outbursts of anger.

As months passed, Mikey's outbursts happened more frequently. Initially he had one in July and two in August. Then, in September, staff documented Mikey's outbursts six times, and in October, eight times. The classroom teacher, Ms. Young, was thorough and methodical in her attempts to intervene and redirect the behavior. Involving the mother in her corrective attempts to soothe and then train new behavior was especially important. If Mikey was going to find new ways of appropriate behavior, coordinating support from home was crucial.

Ms. Stram was supportive right from the start. She made us aware of her turbulent home life and history with her boys' fathers. The three boys had different fathers, and these men were physically and mentally abusive to Ms. Stram and the children. Over the years of abuse, police had been contacted several times and were often in contact with the Stram's family home. The father of each child was currently incarcerated for a major criminal offense. The most important piece of information came when Ms. Stram confided in me that she was currently in psychiatric counseling with the Department of Family Services (DFS). DFS was aware of the nature of the abuse and was providing several resources to wellness for Ms. Stram.

Typically only staff who work directly with a child, like the teacher and aide, are privy to information about past incidents involving abuse, so we were all committed to keeping this information confidential. Our school staff felt shocked after hearing about the Stram family background. We knew that our support would be influential and necessary for this family. When discussing the success of each child's school performance, the home effects of the past and present would also be considered to gain a full, accurate picture.

After hearing about her history of family trauma, the classroom staff developed a soft spot for Ms. Stram. Her life thus far had seemed so destructive, but she remained optimistic and walked confidently through the program site each morning and afternoon to drop off and pick up her children. On the surface, her physical and mental health seemed unaffected by her past. Ms. Stram, a beautiful thirty-two-year-old African American, wore impeccable clothing and was polite each and every day. Everyone marveled at how composed and put together she was.

Yes, the staff not only deeply cared about her children, but they also liked and cherished Ms. Stram. She was always receiving gifts of some kind from staff members. Items like lemons from the backyard tree, gallons of juice, and ice cream treats would be waiting for her upon arrival each day. Word travels quickly throughout a community when the police are routinely called to a specific home. Most staff and community members yearned for life to get better for her.

Unfortunately, after Ms. Stram and Ms. Young began working to correct Mikey's behavior, he began to have more frequent outbursts. I and the staff decided to enlist the support of a new school district resource. Our program was awarded an opportunity to partner with an outside agency, the Mental Health Care Agency (MHCA), which would allow a behavior specialist to work with referred children. The referral process was complete with anecdotal records and a student support team, which would meet to discuss program goals for the child. This outside resource was established to partner with the early childhood division. School personnel feedback identified a growing trend of challenging behaviors in preschool children, which led to the creation of this supportive partnership. Self-promoted as an agency interested in the whole child, it specifically targeted mental health and social-emotional issues.

We set a meeting to welcome the agency professionals and introduce them to my staff. It was pleasant and intentional, as both the MHCA professionals and school staff set intentions for working together to support the needs of a few children at our site. Mikey was immediately placed on the list of students needing this support. Ms. Stram signed the participatory forms, and the support began.

The outside agency professional began observing Mikey and introducing strategies to redirect his behavior when an outburst would occur. Right after the outburst, a rigorous attempt to get Mikey to address his feelings at these moments would ensue. Eventually Mikey's outbursts of arm flailing, biting, and yelling transitioned into subdued words of anger. When the staff would meet to reflect and review his case information, it seemed that progress was occurring. However, we were unprepared for the upcoming three-day event, three days that I never want to relive. Three days that tested the safety of our school structure and systems.

Monday morning began as usual until Ms. Susan, one of the MHCA professionals, approached my office and asked if she could speak with me alone. I welcomed her into my office. Ms. Susan sat on the opposite side of my desk and revealed a student-made drawing, which she placed in front of me. She told me it was Mikey's and that she was very concerned about the drawing. I glanced at the drawing and immediately knew what she was referring to. The picture showed a male with a gun standing over a bloody body. It was so disturbing that at the time I could not even focus on how talented of an artist Mikey was. Based on what I knew of the family's history with violence, the picture was shocking but not surprising.

Because the MHCA professionals worked with multiple children and not just Mikey, they had not been informed of the Stram family's situation. It wasn't until Ms. Susan saw Mikey's drawing that this information was revealed to them. A thorough history was provided to the MHCA so that they could be brought up to speed with this family's history of abuse and violence. After I explained to Ms. Susan that the social service agency and the local police department were very aware of this family's involvement with abuse, she began to understand why the drawing was no surprise. Then Ms. Susan shared something else with me. When she asked Mikey about the people in the drawing, he stated, "My dad has a gun." Mikey went on to explain that his dad was the one in the drawing with the gun and that his mom was on the ground bleeding. Most concerning to Ms. Susan was that Mikey had indicated that this gun was in the house.

At this point, I became alarmed. A phone call was made to the police, and they informed us that Ms. Stram was in fact licensed to have a gun in the house for protection. Apparently she had registered the gun after the last incident involving Mikey's father, an incident that sent him to jail for domestic abuse. We were relieved to hear all of this. Afterward we phoned Ms. Stram to inform her of the drawing. She was saddened to know that Mikey was this emotionally affected by the past events in her home with his dad. She thanked us for our transparency and was willing to support our open communication in working with Mikey's emotions.

Ms. Susan was more hopeful after the phone calls to the authorities and to Mikey's mother. However, she admitted to me that although the local social service agency was aware of this family's history of abuse by the father of these children, she was concerned enough by the drawing to call in a child abuse report.

I felt differently. The drawing was an expression of this child's reaction to several events in the past that he witnessed. Each event was chronicled and documented with the social service agency and with the local authorities. I did not think it was necessary for Ms. Susan to file a report on the matter, and informed Ms. Susan of my stance on the issue.

I was completely blindsided when I arrived at work on Tuesday morning. Upon walking in the door, I was met by my head teacher and office manager. They could not get the words out of their mouths fast enough.

After leaving our campus the day before, Ms. Susan informed her supervisor of the drawing and was directed to call in a child abuse report. The process for calling in a child abuse report is important and, in most cases, necessary. Child abuse reports must be called in to an appropriate child protective agency, either the Department of Children and Family Services or local law enforcement serving the school, and a written report must be filed within thirty-six hours of the call. As mandated reporters, which is what all adults working with children are, we are trained that the employee suspecting child abuse or neglect must make the child abuse telephone report as soon as possible.

Due to the serious repercussions that can occur after making a report, the reporter of an incident may sometimes have doubts as to whether to make a report of child abuse. The philosophy "When in doubt, report" is embedded in all of our trainings and school policy. This philosophy is always mentioned due to gray areas that the person witnessing the alleged abuse may have. If teachers or caregivers see something concerning, they may question themselves before ultimately making the phone call because it is better to be safe than sorry. I believe that is what happened in this case.

To my dismay, the police reacted that evening by removing all three children from the home. At this point, I started to believe that Ms. Susan had omitted the known violent family history to the authorities and social service agencies. This omission would make the situation seem that much more serious and was likely a huge contributor to the children's removal.

My staff knew all of this because Ms. Stram had called that morning to share the events of the night before. During that same phone call, Ms. Stram then told my office manager that she was going to shoot everyone at the school and blow up the building.

After hearing all of this, my mind whirled. What did Ms. Stram hope would happen after making this phone call? What we knew was there had been no incident of violence yet. In my opinion, we had incited the potential violence. I believed Ms. Stram concluded that someone at the school must have called the social service agency and made a child abuse report, which resulted in her children being taken away, a nightmare I am sure she had feared and experienced in the past. She had been so honest and transparent with us. I could only imagine how betrayed, hurt, and helpless she felt. I felt sabotaged by this professional, and I knew I needed to act quickly and confidently to address this explosive moment.

Guns, bombs, and violence were not what I had suited up for when getting dressed that morning. My first step was to call the crisis unit and establish a crisis situation. This triggered our entire school site to transition our facility to "safety" as our highest priority. District personnel, including school police, operations personnel, a school psychologist, and other crisis unit staff were dispersed to our campus due to this threat. A meeting was convened to inform district personnel of the events leading up to the threat, and it was agreed that a phone call to Ms. Stram would be our next course of action. It was decided that as school principal, it would be best if I made the call. Besides, I had a very cordial relationship with Ms. Stram.

The focus of the phone call was to get Ms. Stram to come and meet with us civilly so that we could communicate what had occurred the day before. To my surprise, Ms. Stram answered my call. After I acknowledged her anger, she admitted that she made the threats but in no way was going to carry them out. As she told me this, she cried profusely. I was able to get Ms. Stram to agree to come to the school immediately to discuss the matter. I informed her that school police would have to be called and would be first to greet her upon her arrival.

At this moment, I was told that Ms. Susan, the MHCA professional who triggered all of this, had phoned the school site and informed the office manager that she was not coming to work that day. "Throw the rock and hide," I thought. I was sure that she was aware of the complete mess that was made by that one phone call, which in my opinion should never have been made. This panicked situation caused by our external partner agency was then left at our doorstep to clean up. In my career, there have been moments when well-intended people enter school-site situations (most often in urban areas) and make decisions without considering the professional knowledge of the personnel at that site and the circumstances distinctive to that school community. This was another one of those moments.

None of this should have ever happened, and yet it did. I felt terrible for Ms. Stram and for myself. I was in the strangest of positions. I would have to walk the thin line of confidentiality. I would have to admit our failure in this situation without admitting that it was not our school staff who made the error. What did she think of our school now? She was without a doubt one of our most vocal, supportive parents until this incident happened. Although I was placed in an awkward position, I was confident that my communication skills and prior relationship would soothe the situation and Ms. Stram's anger would subside.

I could not have been more wrong. This incident was shocking, and I was about to be shocked some more.

The meeting was held in our staff lounge that afternoon. The team gathered and began to take their seats as we awaited Ms. Stram's arrival. In the room was district personnel, including a mental health professional, an operations director, a nurse, a head teacher of the site, and Mikey's classroom teacher. Although the MHCA staff personnel were invited, none of them showed up.

To our surprise, Ms. Stram showed up five minutes later. Immediately the atmosphere was tense. Ms. Stram looked completely different than usual. She was not just angry; her physical appearance was different. Most days after dropping off her children, she would head off to work wearing a pantsuit or corporate dress attire. The Ms. Stram who showed up to our meeting was one I did not know. She was wearing dingy sweats, and her hair was half braided and uncombed. She looked odd. I guessed that this befuddled appearance was probably due to not getting sleep the night before, since, after all, her children had just been taken from their home. What time had this occurred? I wondered. How shocking this must have been for her.

As surprising as Ms. Stram's appearance was, there was another surprise: she was not alone. I did not know the woman accompanying her. As they approached, I introduced myself, and the woman said her name was Cheryl. I decided not to ask any questions about this unexpected guest. After all Ms. Stram already thought we had overstepped our boundaries. Ms. Stram and Cheryl entered the meeting, and superficial, strained smiles filled the room. It was silent and tense. The woman who had threatened to blow up the school and shoot staff members sat across from us.

I opened the meeting and asked each person to introduce themselves, then proceeded to summarize the concern of the drawing and events leading up to the children being taken out of the home. I asked Ms. Stram to explain what occurred the night before at her home. Before she even began, tears rolled down her face. I felt terrible, and after surveying the room, I could tell I was not alone in this feeling. What had our school community done? We had victimized a victim.

Ms. Stram started to share the awful events of the night before. She began politely. However, with each sentence, her voice was rising, and it seemed she could barely catch her breath. With tears running profusely down her face, she suddenly, as if out of a movie, rolled back her head, and her eyes widened. She had fainted, or so I thought.

Suddenly Ms. Stram stood up and began to curse. She moved about the room in an aggressive manner. It was at this point that Cheryl called out to her.

"Nicole, calm down." I had never heard someone call Ms. Stram by her first name.

"Shut up," she said, followed by other profane words.

Cheryl took her hands and clapped them right in front of Ms. Stram's face. Ms. Stram collapsed right into Cheryl's arms. Then Cheryl maneuvered herself so she was sitting down with Ms. Stram's head resting in her lap.

Cheryl began to explain why she was attending the meeting. "I'm Cheryl Bronson. I'm a clinical psychiatrist, and I have been working with Ms. Stram. For the past three years, I have been treating Nicole for schizophrenia, and whenever she experiences trauma, what you just saw always shows up. Her worst fear was losing her children, or her children being hurt. In the past, she has witnessed each of her children being burned, hit, and mistreated in countless ways by the men in her life. What you've all witnessed is a loving mother who will do anything to protect her babies. Like a tiger in the night, she will come out of the darkness to strike anyone who hurts them."

Ms. Stram was sobbing with her head still in Cheryl's lap.

"She asked me to come, and we talked all the way over here before we arrived at your school. In the event I was given the chance, she had asked me to say the following. She loves the children's school. She felt such a sense of betrayal by what she perceived to be school-site personnel who were well aware of her family's tragic past, especially because she in fact was the one who shared it."

My mouth was wide open, and the expression on my face was one of awe. Did this just happen right in front of me? I looked around the room, and everyone was stunned. An understanding filled the room. I walked over and put my hands on Ms. Stram's shoulder as she lay in Cheryl's lap. One by one, each person in the room came over and did the same by touching some part of her body or someone in front of them. It was the best group hug I had ever experienced.

Inspired by the moment, I spoke. I prayed out loud for this family. It was not a religious prayer nor particular to any one faith but a prayer for safety and healing for this family. Everyone touched and agreed and felt better after that.

Ms. Stram raised her head and thanked Cheryl for coming and supporting her. Then for one of the few times in my career, I began to weep as Ms. Stram thanked me. What a divine woman, I thought. Thanking me at a time like this was an amazing act of forgiveness.

The rest of that day and the days ahead were filled with reviewing and reflecting on the events that had occurred and the process of our crisis unit team. How had we performed as a school staff in crisis? What steps had been taken to ensure safety at our campus? These and other questions were necessary reflections that had to be assessed, improved, and evaluated based on the answers. One thing was for sure, I would never forget my experience with the Stram family.

This explosive situation had caused us to see ourselves as a school community. Every organization is challenged in this way, and if handled positively, it can be a great impetus for change. The effects of this situation greatly affected our school's dynamic: the staff was reflective, leaders stepped up to the plate to get things done, and the school community questioned itself, which would ultimately lead to more preparation in case of future incidents. Staff planned and attended scenario-based trainings, and we shared the information and lessons learned with parents. The greatest benefit of this entire experience was the feeling of enhanced school safety we mutually shared. We owed that to Ms. Stram!

Coping with Trauma

You don't necessarily need to know the story of a child's trauma or traumatic event to support them. The activities listed below will support coping mechanisms when trauma occurs or build skills to cope before they occur. Trust can take years to build and moments to shatter. Trust can be the difference between a pretty good class and a great class. Building trust can encourage students to open up about their feelings when a negative experience has occurred.

Have children partner up. One partner will be the coach. The other will be blindfolded. Have the coach look at a picture of a face and begin to describe it. The blindfolded child will then use this guidance to draw a picture of the face.

Make a short-term commitment to answer "I don't know" to any questions you may get asked by a child—within reason, of course. Then ask the child to work with you to research an answer. I recommend trying this for a month or two. This helps children develop a strong sense of self as they experience others seeking their help.

Coordinate a wonderful scavenger hunt for the children in your classroom or at home. Form groups and create a list of hidden items, then have children search for them in the environment. This will allow children to work together and develop trust in one another.

Have the children stand in a circle. Then ask them to create a physical human knot by locking their right hand with someone else's right hand in the circle. It works best when the person is on the other side of the circle and not right next to them. Then have them lock left hands with someone else. Now ask them to untangle without unlocking their hands. This is a fun way to build camaraderie.

Ask students to form a line standing side by side. You, the instructor or parent, will then think of a statement with three or four specific details. Quietly share this sentence with the child standing at the beginning of the line. Then instruct that child to whisper the sentence into the ear of the next child and so on. When the sentence is passed all the way to the end of the line, ask the last child to repeat what was said to them. At this point, tell the children what the sentence was supposed to be. After the laughter (because the statement will likely be very different from what was initially said), verbalize the importance of stating only facts when repeating what you have heard. Trust is often earned through the honesty of your statements.

Reflections

☼ When children fear circumstances, what can adults do to assure them in the moment?

☼ How are children affected when they feel trauma? What about adults?

☼ At a time when school shootings have become familiar to us, what do you do to ease fear in children?

☼ What do you do to ensure that children feel safe in your environment?

☼ Can you recall how other professionals have created an atmosphere of safety and trust?

☼ What are the items that contribute to an atmosphere of trust and safety?

☼ What do you need to feel safe?

☼ What makes someone a trustworthy person?

☼ Share a moment when your trust was broken.

☼ Why do you think your family and circle of friends trust you?

12 Gender Identity: The T-Shirt

THE WORLD SEEMS TO HAVE SPED UP, and educators are being asked to keep up, not just with new trends and learnings in academia but also with social factors that influence a child's performance. One instance of this is gender identity. Recently there has been an increase in the number of conversations people are having about gender identity. According to the American Psychological Association (2015), gender identity is a person's deeply felt, inherent sense of being a boy, a man, or male; a girl, a woman, or female; or an alternative gender. I have always been interested in gender identity, but I became especially intrigued after attending a college sociology workshop in my thirties. That workshop helped me realize that most people walking the planet connect sexual identity with gender identity, when in fact they are not related at all.

I learned a lot about gender identity from my friend Veronica. Veronica and I became friends after my college years. She was my only friend at the time who identified as transgender, and she was the first person to help me compartmentalize and separate one's sexual identity from gender. In our culture, sexual identity is tied to gender, but this should not be the case. Your gender does not have anything to do with whom you are attracted to. I was thankful for the knowledge because I have always realized that informing others is a gateway to your freedom and that knowledge for others is a gateway to their understanding.

Gender identity can be very fluid, meaning it may change over time. This is especially common during early childhood because children are developing their personalities and identities. It's important for educators, caregivers, and parents to realize that children love to experiment, role-play, and try new things. They do this with gender as well. While a little girl may identify as a tomboy or a little boy may prefer his sister's dolls to his own toys, it doesn't mean that these children are transgender.

We as educators and parents are increasingly aware that there are students who identify early in their development as a gender other than the one aligned with their sex at birth. Thankfully society at large seems to be moving in an affirmational direction regarding this transition. As educators it is our responsibility to insist that students be affirmed for who they are and to exercise support on behalf of the student making this transition.

Increasing numbers of transgender children are socially transitioning with their gender identity as early as preschool. This may or may not lead to conversations about sexual identity. Any conversations regarding exploration of one's sexuality at an early age should be shared with parents. However, a student undergoing such intense feelings should be supported by the educational system as well. Supporting zero tolerance for bullying and teasing and promoting acceptance and understanding should be the minimum standard. At the very least, teachers should be proactive about making their classroom a safe space for every child.

In the comprehensive guidebook *The Transgender Child*, authors Stephanie A. Brill and Rachel Pepper (2008, 153–54) note that "a child's experience at school can significantly enhance or undermine their sense of self. Furthermore, children need to feel emotionally safe in order to learn effectively. A welcoming and supportive school where bullying and teasing is not permitted and children are actively taught to respect and celebrate difference is the ideal environment for all children. This is especially true for gender-variant and transgender children, who frequently are the targets of teasing and bullying. A child cannot feel emotionally safe, and will most likely experience problems in learning, if they regularly experience discrimination at school." The 2017 National School Climate Survey found that when gender-diverse and sexual-minority youth experienced harassment or assault, almost 60 percent did not report the incident because they believed school staff wouldn't do anything about it (Kosciw et al 2018).

Like the children they teach, educators are constantly learning. They bring whatever life experience and knowledge they have learned with them into their classrooms. Most of my knowledge about gender identity didn't come from the workshop I attended or my friendships; I learned a tremendous amount about gender identity because of a brave child named Tre'.

Tre' was short for Traveon. Tre' was a delightful boy who had just turned three. At the time, I was in my second year as principal of the early education center Tre' attended. In his first year at our site, he was a student in our toddler room. I learned of Tre's uniqueness from a teacher's assistant. She addressed mockingly at first how this new little boy in her class was strangely more feminine than the girls in the class. My stance on the matter was quickly noticed by all staff members as I asked the assistant to elaborate. The tone of my question sent the message that mocking a child's behavior was treading on thin ice. My shift in tone, normally jovial and warm, was immediately recognized by staff as I perused the room at our meeting.

In Tre's first year with us, the staff noticed more and more that he was much different than his male peers. Like most boys his age, Tre' was playful, kind, and smart. Unlike most boys his age, he loved to play with the dolls in the dollhouse, and all of his friends at school were girls. Because Tre' was so young, it was too early for teasing or bullying. I prided myself on ensuring that children felt safe at our center, and Tre' was free to behave how he wished without the pressures of the streets. However, because of my own differentness, I knew that it was only a matter of time before Tre' would face some sort of discrimination.

In the eighties, being black, male, and gay could get you teased, shamed, and possibly beat up at school or in your neighborhood. I was each of these and not happy about the possibility of getting beat up. I remember the feelings of shame and self-doubt. I was different in a world that was not ready to accept me. My successful attempts at fitting in and conforming were satisfying at times, but I paid the price of hiding my true self and suffered from feelings of self-hatred. If it wasn't for supportive parents and a village of wonderful teachers, coaches, and other amazing human beings, I may not have ever turned the corner and gained self-confidence.

My experiences in childhood gave me deep empathy for Tre'. I did not know what Tre's future held, but I felt certain he would face prejudice, and this sparked true compassion from me.

I was not the only one who showed concern for Tre's future. Tre's mother, Ms. Daily, was often visiting the school or calling a teacher to get feedback on his school performance. Her love for her son was evident, but I often wondered if her visitations were the result of her worry.

Ms. Daily was a fascinating woman. She was pleasant and kind to everyone at the school. The staff had come to know her three years prior to Tre's enrollment because of his brother. She was raising her two boys alone as a single mother. Their father was in prison and would be for a long period of time. Tre's brother had matriculated from the early education center and was now in second grade at the adjoining elementary school. His name was Jerome, and he was a rugged boy who loved trucks and sports. Although entirely different, the brothers' affection for each other was solid. Jerome would pick up Tre' occasionally from our school and escort him home. Upon seeing him, Tre' would run up and hug his big brother as if walking home together was the treat of the week. Tre' looked up to Jerome, and Jerome protected Tre'.

At the end of Tre's first year, Ms. Daily approached me and asked if she could speak with me. She was almost apologetic in her delivery. "Of course," I responded.

"Dr. Haggood, I want to thank you. Tre' has had a wonderful year, and I am so glad that he is happy here. I want to speak with you about something very delicate."

"Yes, what is it?" I encouraged.

"Tre' has been asking—no, demanding—that I let him wear girl clothing, and I don't know what to do. I am coming to you because you seem so fair and sensitive with the children. I believe your staff has followed your lead, but to be honest, without you setting the tone here, Tre' might be getting laughed at. I already knew he might be teased and bullied later when I thought he might be gay, but now this. I think he wants to be a girl."

Listening intently I nodded with every sentence to show that I understood and respected her openness. I was amazed at her resilient words. She was coming from such a great place. She shared no judgment of her son with me. Instead she spoke of what she could do to be more understanding and protect her son.

In that moment, I was reminded of my own mother. I knew dealing with my differentness on occasion was not easy for her either. However, like Ms. Daily, her love for me was always apparent.

Ms. Daily and I continued to discuss Tre's gender identity. She shared that her first recognition of Tre' feeling like a girl (I noticed that she replaced "wanting" with "feeling" in her description) was when she saw him tie a T-shirt on his head and wear it around the house. Tre' had been wearing the T-shirt ponytail daily for the past three months. Early attempts to have him take it off resulted in complete meltdowns. She admitted guilt over complying with Tre's desires and wondered out loud if she was in fact encouraging it.

I affirmed her by telling her how exceptional she was. I explained that Tre's feelings were his own, and it sounded like Ms. Daily was seeking understanding of those feelings. I told her that she was setting a great example for Tre' by showing him what he feels matters, and I praised her for providing him with a home where he always felt supported and accepted. The people Tre' valued most were the ones who encouraged him the most. Ms. Daily's compassion had already traveled and been sustained by one child, for Jerome never teased Tre'. On the contrary, if any other kid picked on Tre' verbally or physically in the neighborhood, it was Jerome who would come to the rescue. I wondered how she had become so enlightened as a parent.

I was proud of this family. In what further ways could I support them? I reassured Ms. Daily that as Tre' entered his second year of our program, she could count on us to continue our support of Tre' and his family. I was proud of myself. Although gender identity is a delicate matter for a school and a subject typically not faced in preschool, I could feel within my heart that I was handling this situation with respect and dignity.

It would get more difficult in Tre's final year with us. He was four and in prekindergarten. In the first month of the new year, Ms. Daily came to meet with me. She mentioned that the family was in counseling to support Tre' and that he was now dressing completely as a girl at home. She mentioned that when they went shopping, she faced rolled eyes and aggressive words from family and friends if Tre' tried on girls' clothes at the store. When Ms. Daily tearfully shared this with me, it was the first time I had seen her cry. She admitted that she dreaded going shopping because of the public humiliation she had to endure.

Ms. Daily shared this with me because she had come into my office to ask about the ramifications of allowing Tre' to come to school dressed in girls' clothing. I assured her that the adult staff at our school always spoke of our site as a safe zone. We had no tolerance for teasing or demeaning children; it was one of our most important priorities. I promised her that this commitment would not change and told her that if she decided that it was in Tre's best interest to allow him to dress differently, I would support her decision as the leader of the school.

Had I spoken too soon? Was my staff ready for this? I asked after she left. The answers were "yes" to the former and "no" to the latter. I decided to meet with my staff and transparently discuss Ms. Daily's possible future decision to send Tre' to school in girls' clothing. After I shared this with them, the fear in the room was immediate yet understandable. They asked questions like "What will other parents think and say?" and "What influence will this have on the other children?" I assured them that Ms. Daily did not want this change to begin immediately. This allowed each of us time to learn more about the subject matter.

Soon after the meeting, I scheduled two workshops on gender identity with my staff. The workshops included a presentation by speakers from our district's antibias unit. These speakers had knowledge of various subject matter related to supporting groups who face discrimination. So much information was presented to staff in the workshops. There was a lot to learn, but digesting vocabulary terms quickly was not the goal—the goal was to make Tre' feel loved. After gauging the expressive faces of the staff, I determined that the majority were on the same page in our efforts to handle this tough situation. I was so proud of my staff that year.

Tre' never came to school dressed in girls' clothing. Ms. Daily decided against it. It made life more tolerable for the family, and Tre' was loved regardless. This was still a positive experience, for I am encouraged whenever I am surrounded by professionals who put children first. Even though we did not have many answers for what seems to be an increasingly common subject, the staff and I learned numerous valuable lessons. Now when I encounter a situation that cannot be resolved by a policy because that policy does not exist, I remind myself that my school-site decision should always be based on a child's best interest, period. Thanks, Tre'!

Let Me Be Me!

Ask students to make an image collage of typical and nontypical behavior by using photos found in magazines. Typical and nontypical examples will be given to children. (Traditional and nontraditional can also be used as identifiers when making the collage.) For instance, an image of a girl wearing feminine clothing could be juxtaposed with an image of a girl wearing more masculine clothing. The purpose of this activity is to help students discover that they hold ideas about what boys and girls should do and be, and it allows them to identify ways they can break these molds themselves.

Have children list the characteristics of four marine animals: shark, dolphin, octopus, and crab. After listing the traits of each marine animal, students will be asked to discuss times in which they behaved like each of these animals. The purpose of this activity is to help students understand that we are complex and will exhibit each creature's characteristics at different times. Remind students that all these communication styles can be valuable, but it is most beneficial to our society if we communicate in ways that show support, peace, and social justice.

Have the students divide into small groups. Ask them to construct a home with materials you provide. The students will work together to make a home and identify roles of family members living in the home. Each home will look different, and each family will be different. The purpose of this exercise should become apparent to students, although you should elaborate by reminding them that while each home is constructed differently, the family inside of the home is where the value lies.

Display pictures of adults who don't conform to traditional gender roles. Ask children to state positive affirmations of what they see. List these comments on butcher paper below each picture so that old and traditional societal perceptions are not the only messages observed.

Ask children to write or talk about a time when they felt different. Next ask them to list some similarities they have with other students in the class. This "alike" list will then be shared with the group. Compare and contrast to share the empowering message that we are all different and alike in many ways and that no one should be shamed for who they are.

Reflections

☼ How can you support children who don't conform to traditional gender roles?

☼ What are children most likely to do when they are forced to conform to what adults want?

☼ What are the alternatives to insisting that a child conform to a school dress code?

☼ How can we display acceptance in learning communities?

☼ How can we affirm open-minded environments?

☼ What do developmentally preschool-age children learn about boys and girls?

☼ When a child is internally developing feelings around gender, what can adults do to support that child?

☼ What would you like children to learn about gender?

☼ What can children teach us about responding to change?

☼ What do you do when you find yourself judging others?

Discussion Questions and Book Club Guidance

These questions are meant to serve as a guide for parents, teachers, or administrators interested in reading and discussing the text and context of *Let Them Shine*. In order to have a productive and enjoyable conversation, we recommend keeping a few guidelines in mind.

Appointing a moderator is a great way to make sure that the group has guidance and direction. It is best if the moderator is appointed before the day of the meeting/discussion since they will then be able to read over the questions ahead of time and prepare mentally to facilitate the conversation for all involved. While they should not be a conversational tyrant, it is important that their role as group head be clear to and respected by all involved.

The questions listed here are starting points, not requirements. They can be used instead of or in conjunction with the "Reflections" questions at the end of each chapter. If the conversation begins to move organically in another direction (within the realm of relevancy to the issues at hand, of course), it is often most interesting and useful to allow the digression. It is often productive to leave time at the end of the designated block for questions that the participants came up with while reading. Whether factual or open-ended, clarification of these queries helps build a group mentality and gives your discussion unique flavor.

Most of all, it is important that all group members feel welcome and that their opinions and experiences are treated with empathy. This basic rule fosters dialogue and, when made clear at the outset, helps create a sense of safety within the space of the discussion.

Questions for general discussion:

☼ How did you come to this book? Did you feel burnt out, in need of inspiration? Did you find inspiration?

☼ Which story hit closest to home for you, whether due to a similar experience with a student/child or in your own life?

☼ Were there stories where you would have reacted differently than the author did?

☼ Share an inspirational anecdote from your own career or time parenting.

☼ Was there an educator that you particularly looked up to in your early life?

Story-based questions:

☼ Chapter 1: What do you think of Ms. Bream's strategy?

☼ Chapter 2: Is there a particular book that has been impactful in your life or classroom?

☼ Chapter 3: How do you deal with failure? How do you model this for the children in your life?

☼ Chapter 4: Have you personally witnessed a moment of compassion or class-wide empathy similar to this example? How do group dynamics in your classroom affect the way children view themselves and their place in the group relative to their lives outside it?

☼ Chapter 5: Have you ever been confronted with an instance of the gendered understanding of childhood? Is there one you've been trying to gather the courage to confront?

☼ Chapter 6: Do you feel the same way about your body that you did when you were young? To what extent did parents/teachers/other adult authority figures contribute to your self-image?

☼ Chapter 7: How have you encountered the different attitudes and cultures around teaching in different environments (urban, suburban, rural)?

☼ Chapter 8: How do you deal with bad behavior that shows a spark of genius like Faith's did?

☼ Chapter 9: How do you use humor to bond in a way that is age appropriate?

☼ Chapter 10: Is there someone who has led you to question the "why" of school life?

References

Agency for Healthcare and Quality. 2009. "Hospitalizations for Eating Disorders from 1999 to 2006." Agency for Healthcare and Quality. www.hcup-us.ahrq.gov/reports/statbriefs/sb70.pdf.

American Psychological Association. 2015. "Key Terms and Concepts in Understanding Gender Diversity and Sexual Orientation Among Students." American Psychological Association. www.apa.org/pi/lgbt/programs/safe-supportive/lgbt/key-terms.pdf.

Brill, Stephanie A., and Rachel Pepper. 2008. *The Transgender Child: A Handbook for Families and Professionals*. San Francisco: Cleis Press.

Eiseley, Loren C. 1978. *The Star Thrower*. New York: Times Books.

Gallivan, Heather. 2014. *Teens, Social Media and Body Image*. Park Nicollet Melrose Center. www.macmh.org/wp-content/uploads/2014/05/18_Gallivan_Teens-social-media-body-image-presentation-H-Gallivan-Spring-2014.pdf.

Kindlon, Dan, and Michael Thompson. 2000. *Raising Cain: Protecting the Emotional Life of Boys*. New York: Ballantine Books.

Kosciw, Joseph G., Emily A. Greytak, Adrian D. Zongrone, Caitlin M. Clark, and Nhan L. Truong. 2018. *The 2017 National School Climate Survey: The Experiences of Lesbian, Gay, Bisexual, Transgender, and Queer Youth in Our Nation's Schools*. New York: GLSEN.

Rothman, Lily. 2017. "How Title IX First Changed the World of Women's Sports." *Time*. June 23. www.time.com/4822600/title-ix-womens-sports.

Sears, Bill. 2018. "12 Ways to Raise a Confident Child." Ask Dr. Sears. Accessed March 29. www.askdrsears.com/topics/parenting/child-rearing -and-development/12-ways-help-your-child-build-self-confidence.

US Census Bureau. 2012. "Family Structure and Children's Living Arrangements." Current Population Report. US Census Bureau. www2 .ed.gov/rschstat/statistics/surveys/mbk/Family-structure_verified.xlsx.